FIFTY VOICES OF
THE TWENTIETH CENTURY

FIFTY VOICES of the TWENTIETH CENTURY

Selected by EMERY KELEN

Lothrop, Lee & Shepard Co. ⚓ New York

76-2291

The material quoted on pages 44 to 46 is from
The Basic Writings of Sigmund Freud, translated
and edited by Dr. A. A. Brill. Copyright © 1938
by Random House, Inc. Copyright renewed 1965
by Gioia B. Bernheim and Edmund R. Brill.
Reprinted by permission.

The author is also grateful to
Houghton Mifflin Company for permission
to quote from *The Human Use of Human
Beings* by Norbert Wiener. Material from
Out of My Life and Thought
by Albert Schweitzer, translated
by C. T. Campion, copyright 1933, 1949,
© 1961 by Holt, Rinehart and Winston, Inc.,
is reprinted with the permission of
Holt, Rinehart and Winston, Inc.

ALSO BY EMERY KELEN

✣ | *Let's Learn About the United Nations*
Proverbs of Many Nations

CONTENTS

INTRODUCTION

These are the thoughts of some of the great men and women of our time—selected artists, writers, politicians, philosophers, and scientists. They express their opinions on a variety of subjects, and sometimes these opinions contradict each other. After the words of a pacifist, for instance, you might find those of a war maker. Therefore, while many of these people saw their obligations to their fellow men in a highly ethical light, I have picked certain other quotations in order to make the reader aware of his own national and international responsibilities. And, of course, some quotes are here simply because they are amusing and delightful.

Emery Kelen

MARIAN ANDERSON

☧ *American-Negro contralto. She was born in Philadel-phia, in 1908. Her absorbing interest since childhood* has been music. Accepted for instruction by teachers of increasing distinction, she won a contest at Lewisohn Stadium in New York and sang at Carnegie Hall. After studying abroad and successfully touring Europe, she then completely won her homeland, and has sung to capacity audiences ever since.

In 1939 she was awarded the Spingarn Medal, presented annually to the American Negro of "highest achievement."

Marian Anderson's claim to world fame lies in her extraordinary voice, which embraces more than two octaves and moves her hearers to the marrow of their bones. She is taller than she appears in her photographs—about five feet eight—but her broad shoulders make her seem stockier than she is.

One look at Marian Anderson brings an awareness that here is a complete human being who has the inner guidance of spiritual excellence, intellect, and intuition. At no time do her religious ardor and the fullness of her heart, with its tenderness, passion, and power, come to better expression than when she closes her eyes, cramps her fingers, stiffens her neck, and sings a Negro spiritual. At such times she undergoes a religious experience, and so do her listeners.

Marian Anderson was United States delegate to the United Nations Trusteeship, an organization that works for the betterment of some 130,000,000 black people in the dark corners of the world. No more inspired person ever occupied a delegate's chair!

. . . . .

There are great areas where people overseas need to know and meet equivalent people in America. There are so many misconceptions.

The main feeling is that America has a lot of money and is attempting to buy what it likes. A lot of people don't want to be bought.

We give people what we think they ought to have, not what they should have. One mustn't give people things because we happen to think they need them. The important thing is to find out what they really need.

Cities were dots on maps, far away and terribly sort of impersonal, you know. Then one goes there and sees the buildings and the seething mobs of people, and sings to them, and also talks to people as intelligent as one finds anywhere. Naturally one comes away with different ideas.

JAMES BALDWIN

American-Negro author, born in New York's Harlem in 1924, the son of a Baptist preacher. In his early life he tried to avoid association with Negroes. For years he refused to eat watermelon, because watermelon eating was associated with the image of the Negro child. In his child-hood, he recalls, "One's hair was always being attacked with hard brushes and combs and Vaseline; it was shameful to have 'nappy' hair. One's legs and arms and face were always being greased, so that one would not look 'ashy' in the wintertime. One was always being mercilessly scrubbed and polished, as though in the hope that a stain could thus be washed away. . . . The women were forever straightening and curling their hair, and using bleaching creams, and yet it was clear that none of this would release one from the stigma of being a Negro; this effort merely increased the shame and rage."

Author Baldwin is a slight, nervous, passionate man. He does none of the things usually associated with Negro leaders. He preaches from no pulpit and does not devise plans for sit-ins. His strength lies, not in being a Black Power advocate or a racist, but in his articles, pamphlets, and books, where he is a bitter critic of white Americans.

. . . . .

At the root of the American-Negro problem is the necessity of the American white man to find a way of living with the Negro in order to be able to live with himself.

In this long battle, the white man's motive was the protection of his identity; the black man was motivated by the need to establish an identity.

Uncle Tom is, for example, if he is called Uncle, a kind of saint. He is there, he endures, he will forgive us, and this is a key to that image. But if he is not Uncle, if he is merely Tom he is a danger to everybody.

We [should] never victimize as we do, children whose only crime is color.

We [shouldn't] drive Negroes mad as we do by accepting them in ballparks, and on concert stages, but not in our homes, and not in our neighborhoods, and not in our churches.

I do not know many Negroes who are eager to be "accepted" by white people, still less to be loved by them; they, the blacks, simply don't wish to be beaten over the head by the whites every instant of our brief passage on this planet.

Negro servants have been smuggling odds and ends out of white homes for generations, and white people have been delighted to have them do it, because it has assuaged a dim guilt and testified of the intrinsic superiority of white people.

In any case, white people, who had robbed black people of their liberty and who profited by this theft every hour that they lived, had no moral ground on which to stand.

It seems to be indispensable to the national self-esteem that the Negro be considered either as a kind of ward, or as a victim.

All racists are irresponsible.

White Americans find it as difficult as white people elsewhere do to divest themselves of the notion that they are in possession of some intrinsic value that black people need, or want.

I beg the black people of this country to do something which I know to be very difficult: to be proud of the auction block, and all that rope, and all that fire, and all that pain.

DAVID BEN-GURION

✞ *David Ben-Gurion was born in Plonsk, Poland, in 1886. His constant dream was that one day Palestine* would become a Jewish homeland, and in 1906, when he was twenty years old, he immigrated to Palestine, which in those days was under Turkish rule.

At first Ben-Gurion worked on a farm. Later he helped to establish the Palestine Labor Party, and wrote articles under the pen name of Ben-Gurion, "The Lion's Cub." The name is significant, because he selected it as fitting his personality.

He studied law in Constantinople, now Istanbul, but was expelled by the Turkish authorities in 1915. During World War I he came to the United States and set up an organization to encourage immigration to Palestine, and helped to organize the Jewish Legion of Volunteers, who fought alongside the British against the Turks in the Holy Land.

When, on October 1, 1947, the United Nations General Assembly voted the partition of Palestine into separate Jewish and Arab states, Ben-Gurion was at Lake Success to watch the proceedings. By May 15, 1948, Britain pulled her troops out of Palestine, and the newborn Israel was promptly invaded by Jordan, Lebanon, and Egypt. After nine months of war, an armistice was arranged by Ralph

Bunche of the United Nations, but no peace treaty was concluded. Today, several wars later, there still is none.

Ben-Gurion's spiritual roots lie in the Bible, but he reads widely on philosophy and science, and enjoys a good argument. As leader of the Mapai, the Labor Party, he was the first Premier of Israel.

.   .   .   .   .

I have learned one thing from the appalling atrocities of Hitler: to make every possible effort to prevent such a disaster falling on the people of Israel. For although Hitler was defeated, his disciples in the Middle East still live, and it is they who rule in the Arab countries that surround us.

We, more than any other nation, need friends.

It is our duty to adopt all measures to safeguard our peace and security.

Faith is much more important than arms or riches or numbers. It is our real weapon.

GEORGE WASHINGTON CARVER

✥ | *This American-Negro botanist lived one of the most*
| *fruitful as well as one of the most adventurous of lives.*
His birth date is not known exactly, but it is estimated to
be 1864. His mother was a slave at the Carver plantation,
near Diamond Grove, Missouri.

At the time the Civil War was raging. Southern soldiers
raided the plantation and carried off the slave woman and
her newborn babe. Farmer Carver gathered a rescue party,
overtook the captors and, offering them a broken-down
horse in trade, was able to get the child back. His mother,
however, disappeared without leaving a trace.

Farmer Carver named the fragile little boy George Washington. After the war ended, he had no money to give him
for his education, so the boy learned to cook, knit, and
crochet. What he liked most, though, was to wander in the
woods, talk to the flowers, and make beautifully colored
drawings of plants. He earned money as a singer, ran a
laundry, and served as a church organist.

To support himself while he was going to high school, he
worked as a dishwasher, laundryman, and housekeeper. He
then obtained a Bachelor's Degree in Science at the Iowa

State College at Ames, where he also took his Master's Degree in 1896.

Because of his unusual talent, George Washington Carver was given a place on the faculty at Ames, a very rare honor for a Negro in those days. And then Dr. Booker T. Washington offered him a job at the Tuskegee Institute. The salary was meager, laboratory facilities nonexistent, but Dr. Carver left Ames and came. Soon he had a laboratory set up, using discarded bottles and other rejects rescued from junk heaps.

He established an experimental farm of nineteen acres on the worst land in Alabama. The first year it brought him a net loss of $16.25 per acre, but scientific treatment and cultivation improved its production. In a couple of years he was netting a profit of $40 an acre.

His chief work was with the peanut and the sweet potato, for both of which he discovered hundreds of new uses. He also achieved remarkable results with pecans, cotton, cornstalks, and even ordinary weeds.

Dr. Carver was a god-fearing man. His temple was the forest, from which he always brought back large bunches of rare flowers. He felt God put things in an environment for a reason. Therefore, he went out—and taught his students to go out—and gathered from an apparently thankless land whatever was needed.

Dr. Carver, who died in 1943, gave his life savings to the Carver Research Laboratories. He was certainly one of the great geniuses given to the world by the Negro race.

· · · · ·

I talk to the peanut and the sweet potato and the clays of the hills, and they talk back to me. Here great wonders are brought forth.

There is literally nothing that I ever wanted to do, that I asked the blessed Creator to help me to do, that I have not been able to accomplish.

It's all very simple, if one knows how to talk with the Creator. It is simply seeking the Lord and finding Him.

All my life I have risen regularly at four o'clock and have gone into the woods and talked with God. There He gives me my orders for the day.

When people are still asleep I hear God best and learn my plan.

After my morning's talk with God I go into my laboratory and begin to carry out His wishes for the day.

No books are ever brought in here [to the laboratory] and what is the need of books? Here I talk to the little peanut and it reveals its secrets to me.

On every Saturday afternoon my infantile paralysis patients come in a steady stream from one o'clock until bed time, and I haven't a minute to myself. I hold that day and Sunday sacred for them. I invite them all to come—unless it rains.

Anything will give up its secrets if you love it enough. Not only have I found that when I talk to the little flower or to the little peanut they will give up their secrets, but I have found that when I silently commune with people they give up their secrets also—if you love'them enough.

The great Creator gave us three kingdoms, the animal, the vegetable, and the mineral. Now he has added a fourth, the synthetic kingdom.

It is going to be a great revival of Christianity, not a revival of religion. We can have religion and still have wars. But this is to be a revival of *true* Christianity. It is going to rise from the laymen, from men who are going about their work and putting God into what they do, from men who believe in prayer, and who want to make God real to mankind.

When I touch that flower, I am not merely touching that flower, I am touching infinity. That little flower existed long before there were human beings on this earth. It will continue to exist for thousands, yes, millions of years to come.

What is the Infinite? It is that silent, small force. It isn't the outer physical contact. No, it isn't that. The infinite is not confined in the visible world. It is not in the earthquake, the wind, or the fire. It is that still small voice that calls up the fairies.

There are certain things, often very little things, like the little peanut, the little piece of clay, the little flower, that cause you to look *within*—and then it is that you see into the soul of things.

The soul cannot be measured out. The soul is infinite. I am not trying to describe the soul, but the soul is all that we have that is worth living for—all that we have. You take that away and we become worse than the beasts in the field.

And I know that there is nothing more pitiful than meeting the little bodies of those that get no further than their little selves, people who can't get away from the little "I," people who are afflicted with the "I disease," the worst of all the diseases.

WINSTON CHURCHILL

British statesman, historian, war leader, author, lecturer—and in his free time painter and bricklayer— he was truly as versatile as a man of the Renaissance.

He was born in 1874—prematurely. His American-born mother was at a dance in the ancestral castle of Blenheim when baby Winston gave signs of impatience. She ran toward her bedroom, but only got as far as the ladies' cloakroom. There he was born. "Most unconventional," remarked the Duchess of Marlborough. And Winston grew up to be a most unconventional person.

The routine education of the time did not bring out Winston's qualities. He went to Sandhurst for training to become a soldier, and served three years with a cavalry regiment in India. In 1899 he went to South Africa as a journalist, reporting the Boer War for the *Morning Post.* There he was taken prisoner by the Boers, but made a spectacular escape. In 1900 he began his political career, entering the House of Commons. In 1908 he joined the Cabinet, as President of the Board of Trade.

The outbreak of World War I in 1914 found Churchill at the head of the Admiralty. When, in 1915, the Allied and German armies were bogged down in the mud of France and Flanders, Churchill, in order to break the dead-lock, devised a plan of turning the enemy's flank and attack-ing the Dardanelles. The enterprise ended up as one of the great disasters of the war for the Allies. As a result of this failure, Churchill was dismissed from the Admiralty, and he made penance by serving with the army in France. Not until two years later was he again admitted into the Cab-inet of Lloyd George.

In 1930, after a sharp disagreement with the Conserva-tive Party, he was excluded from their ranks for the next ten years. During that time he made a living by lecturing and writing books.

Then on September 1, 1939, Germany invaded Poland. Two days later, Britain and France declared war on Ger-many. That same day, Churchill joined the government as First Lord of the Admiralty. On May 10, 1940, Prime Min-ister Neville Chamberlain resigned, and the King invited Churchill, as Prime Minister, to form a new Cabinet.

By then, Norway, Denmark, Holland, and Belgium had fallen to Hitler. At Dunkirk the British army was hurled into the sea, all its equipment lost. The French army col-lapsed and Italy entered the war. Britain stood alone. This was Churchill's finest hour. With eloquence and courage he held the British people together, and they withstood Germany.

Then, on December 7, 1941, the Japanese attack on Pearl Harbor brought the United States into the war. Churchill negotiated with President Roosevelt the alliance that, together with Russia, eventually defeated Germany,

Italy, and Japan, and led to the founding of the United Nations.

In March, 1946, in an address to Westminster College in Fulton, Missouri, he warned against the Communist take-over in Europe. It was the declaration of the "cold war." Stalin's paper *Pravda* denounced him as an "anti-Soviet warmonger" and compared him to Hitler.

In 1955 he retired from politics. He died in 1965.

. . . . .

I have nothing to offer but blood, toil, tears, and sweat.

We shall defend our island, whatever the cost may be, we shall fight on the beaches, we shall fight on the landing grounds, we shall fight in the fields and in the streets, we shall fight in the hills; we shall never surrender.

You Hitler, do your worst, and we shall do our best.

Come on, we shall easily devour your entire hostile horde!

Let us therefore brace ourselves to our duties, and so bear ourselves that, if the British Empire and its Commonwealth last for a thousand years, men will still say, "This was their finest hour."

(December 26, 1941, before the joint session of Congress:) I cannot help reflecting that if my father had been American and my mother British instead of the other way around, I might have gotten here on my own. In that case, this would not have been the first time you would have heard my voice. In that case, I should not have needed an invitation, but if I had, it is hardly likely it would have been unanimous.

(In Fulton, Missouri:) A shadow has fallen upon the scenes so lately lighted by the Allied victory. . . . From Stettin in the Baltic to Trieste in the Adriatic an iron curtain has descended across the Continent.

We hope to reach again a Europe purged of the slavery of ancient days in which men will be as proud to say "I am a European" as once they were to say "Civis Romanus sum" (I am a Roman citizen).

As life unfolds I have been astonished to find how many more degrees I have received than I have passed examinations. I was never very good at those.

It is a Socialist idea that making profit is a vice; I consider the real vice is making losses.

Russia is a riddle wrapped in a mystery inside an enigma.

Both honor and wisdom demand that Israel should be preserved.

As long . . . as the free world holds together, and especially Britain and the United States, and maintains its strength, Russia will find that Peace and Plenty have more to offer than exterminatory war.

I am ready to meet my Maker. Whether my Maker is prepared for the great ordeal of meeting me is another matter.

Parliament can compel people to obey or to submit, but it cannot compel them to agree.

It is not Parliament that should rule; it is the people who should rule through Parliament.

The object of Parliament is to substitute argument for fisticuffs.

The foundation of all democracy is that the people have the right to vote. To deprive them of that right is to make a mockery of all the high-sounding phrases which are so often used. At the bottom of all the tributes paid to democracy is the little man, walking into the little booth, with a little pencil, making a little cross on a little bit of paper— no amount of rhetoric or voluminous discussion can possibly diminish the overwhelming importance of that point.

The inherent vice of Capitalism is the unequal sharing of blessings; the inherent value of Socialism is the equal sharing of miseries.

For my part, I consider that it will be found much better by all parties to leave the past to history, especially as I propose to write that history myself.

It is a fine thing to be honest, but it is also very important to be right.

Never in the field of human conflict was so much owed by so many to so few.

(Commenting on the opinion of French generals who told their government that, "In three weeks England will have her neck wrung like a chicken.") Some chicken! Some neck!

Come on now all you young men, all over the world. . . . Twenty to twenty-five! These are the years! Don't be content with things as they are. "The earth is yours and the fulness thereof." Enter upon your inheritance, accept your responsibilities. Raise the glorious flags again, advance them upon the new enemies, who constantly gather upon the front of the human army, and have only to be assaulted to be overthrown. . . . You will make all kinds of mistakes; but as long as you are generous and true, and also fierce, you cannot hurt the world or even seriously distress her. She was made to be wooed and won by youth. She has lived and thrived only by repeated subjugations.

AARON COPLAND

Aaron Copland, American composer and lecturer, was born in Brooklyn, New York, in 1900. He has been acclaimed the "Dean of American Composers," for he is their leading spirit. He works untiringly to promote an understanding of the new music and to secure hearings for his colleagues.

He was the first American to study composition in Paris, where his teacher was Nadia Boulanger, the famous teacher, conductor, and organist. He became a lecturer at the New School for Social Research in New York City, and at Harvard, and taught composition at the Berkshire Music Center. Some of his best-known works are inspired by folklore, especially the ballets, *Rodeo, Billy the Kid*, and *Appalachian Spring*. He has composed symphonies, chamber music, choral works, a concerto for piano and orchestra, and much film music, such as *The City, Of Mice and Men, Our Town, North Star, The Red Pony*, and *The Heiress*.

His articles are mostly on contemporary music. A series of lectures he gave was published as a book—*What to Listen for in Music*. Other books are *Copland on Music* and *Music and Imagination*.

. . . . .

The "problem" of listening to a fugue by Handel is essentially no different from that of listening to a similar work by Hindemith.

If you want to understand music better, you can do nothing more important than listen to it.

The simplest way of listening to music is to listen for the sheer pleasure of the musical sound itself.

The important thing is that each one feel for himself the specific expressive quality of a theme or, similarly, an entire piece of music.

The playwright creates and develops a character in just the same way that a composer creates and develops a theme.

Someone once asked me . . . whether I waited for inspiration. My answer was: "Every day!"

A musical idea is not the same as a piece of music. It only induces a piece of music.

A beautiful melody, like a piece of music in its entirety . . . must give us a sense of completion and of inevitability.

To stop the flow of music would be like the stopping of time itself, incredible and inconceivable.

To some African tribes rhythm *is* music, they have nothing

more. But what rhythm it is! . . . It seems inexact and even unfair to call them primitive.

The art of orchestration . . . holds endless fascination for the practicing composer, being part science and part guesswork.

Color in music, as in painting, is meaningful only when it serves the expressive idea.

Music strikes us in as many different ways as there are composers, and anything less than a strong reaction, pro or con, is not worth bothering about.

What strikes me most markedly about Bach's work is the marvelous rightness of it. It is the rightness not merely of a single individual but of a whole musical epoch.

Beethoven is one of the great yea-sayers among creative artists; it is exhilarating to share his clear-eyed contemplation of the tragic sum of life.

In the musical field there appears to be an unquenchable thirst for the familiar, and very little curiosity as to what the newer composers are up to.

ILYA G. EHRENBURG

☦ | *Soviet cosmopolitan writer. The term* cosmopolitan *is not a compliment in the Soviet Union. He was born* in 1891, into a Jewish middle-class family. In World War I he served on the Western Front as a correspondent for a St. Petersburg financial newspaper. When the revolution broke out in 1917, he went home to Russia, but had no place in the Bolshevik revolution.

Most of the time he lived on the Montparnasse in Paris where, in the Café du Dome, he was a familiar figure, stooped, unshaven, with newspapers and books under his arm. Mrs. Ehrenburg was as elegant as her husband was sloppy. He fled when the Nazis occupied Paris in 1940, and described the events in his book *The Fall of Paris*, which won the Stalin Prize in 1942.

In 1946, he toured the United States for two months with two other Soviet journalists, and reported his impressions in *Collier's* magazine.

Ehrenburg was often accused of being an opportunist, catering to every political trend. Certainly he lived in difficult times, when speaking one's mind was dangerous to life and freedom. He did his best, circumstances permitting.

He died in 1967 at the age of seventy-six.

. . . . .

There are pedigreed dogs and there are mongrels, both good in their own ways. I would say that a mongrel is more of an all-rounder than a pedigreed animal, which is rather like a human specialist.

I want to believe that the American people will find in themselves the strength of spirit, the perception and wisdom to say to the people who are preparing for a third world war: "Enough! I do not intend to pay for your ink with my blood."

There is nothing more wonderful than freedom of speech.

My memories are anything but a dispassionate chronicle.

Modern European and American literature is unthinkable without the classical Russian novel.

Many of America's qualities and defects are due to her age.

An author is not a piece of machinery, mechanically registering events. . . . An author does not write a book because he has to earn a living. An author writes a book because he finds it necessary to tell people something of himself, because he is pregnant with his book, because he has seen people, things, and emotions that he cannot help describing.

That is why I cannot understand some critics when they

blame such-and-such a writer: he has not written a novel about the Volga-Don canal, about the textile industry, or about the struggle for peace. Would it not be better to reproach another author, who has written a book, although he felt no spiritual compulsion to do so and could have quietly left it unwritten?

In pre-revolutionary times an author's life was not an easy one, and in Chekhov's letters there is mention of how the editors of a newspaper or magazine would order a story from him. But even the most impudent of editors refrained from suggesting to Chekhov the subject of his story. Can one imagine Tolstoi being given an instruction to write *Anna Karenina* or Gorki being ordered to write *Mother*?

ALBERT EINSTEIN

✝ | *German-born American scientist, who at the age of twenty-six rang up the curtain on the atomic age.* His was one of the greatest minds in history. His theories will eventually change the thinking of man about himself and about his fellowmen; they have already changed the ways of warfare.

He was born in 1879, in Ulm, Germany. His father was a dealer in electrical supplies. Albert gave no early sign of genius: he was slow to talk and slower to read. His teachers labeled him dull and stupid.

As a teen-ager, young Albert began to manifest an amazing propensity for science and mathematics, and he decided to make them his career. He studied at a technical school in Zurich, and afterward found work in the International Patent Office in Berne. The job did not pay well, and he passed a miserable four years in poverty and ill health, but in his spare time he was able to pursue his studies.

In 1905 he published in a scientific journal his famous formula, $E = mc^2$. The formula meant that small quantities of mass were capable of producing tremendous amounts of energy.

From then on, the eyes of the scientific world were on

him. Einstein left his patent-office job to teach. He taught at the universities in Berne, Zurich, and Prague and, finally, at the University of Berlin.

In 1921, anti-Semitic riots broke up his lectures. Charges were brought against him that, as a Jew, he was deliberately trying to mislead the world with nonsense.

The tide of Nazism rose. When Hitler came to power, Einstein left Germany. He went to France, Belgium, and England and, in October, 1933, he arrived in the United States, where he became a member of the faculty of the Institute for Advanced Study at Princeton. In 1940 he became an American citizen, having settled into the modest and quiet life of a shy college professor.

Because there was a danger that Germany might develop the atom bomb, Einstein wrote a letter of warning to President Roosevelt on August 2, 1939, and the Government took heed. A two-billion-dollar fund was set up to develop the bomb. Six years after Einstein's letter, almost to the very day, on August 6, 1945, an American atom bomb exploded over Japan. Personally, he was in favor of outlawing the use of the bomb.

Few people know that Einstein also contributed to the development of television. He discovered the photoelectric law, which won him the Nobel Prize in 1922. The application of this law led eventually to the creation of the photoelectric cell and to television.

Einstein died in 1955 at the age of seventy-six. Although the last words of great men are cherished by posterity, his will never be known, because the nurse who attended him couldn't speak German.

. . . . .

Out yonder, there was this huge world, which exists independently of us human beings . . . the contemplation of this world beckons like a liberation.

If my theory is proven correct, Germany will hail me as a great German and the French will hail me as a citizen of the world. If it is proven false, the French will call me a German and the Germans will call me a Jew.

I refuse to make money out of science . . . my laurel is not for sale.

Let every man be respected as an individual and no man idolized.

I believe that whoever tries to think things through honestly will soon recognize how unworthy and even fatal is the traditional bias against Negroes. . . . What can the man of good will do to combat this deeply rooted prejudice? He must have the courage to set an example by words and deed, and must watch lest his children become influenced by racial bias.

As long as I have my choice, I will stay only in a country where political liberty, toleration and equality of all citizens before the law are the rule. . . . Political liberty implies liberty to express one's political opinions orally or in writing, and a tolerant respect for any and every individual opinion.

Since the arrival of the Fascist danger, I for the present no longer believe in the effectiveness of the absolute passive pacifism. As long as Fascism rules in Europe, there will be no peace.

Had I known that the Germans would not succeed in developing an atomic bomb, I would have done nothing for the bomb.

The armament race is the worst method to prevent open conflict. . . . It should not be forgotten that the atomic bomb was made in this country as a preventive measure. . . . A refusal to outlaw the use of the bomb . . . is hardly pardonable.

Nationalism is an infantile disease. It is the measles of mankind.

Taking an active part in the solution of the problems of peace is a moral duty which no conscientious man can shirk.

A leading point of view of all political action should . . . be: what can we do to bring about a peaceful coexistence and even loyal cooperation of the nations?

Our schoolbooks glorify war and hide its horrors. They inculcate hatred in the veins of the children. I would teach peace rather than war. I would inculcate love rather than hate.

The release of atomic energy has not created a new problem. It has merely made more urgent the necessity of solving an existing one. . . . A new type of thinking is essential if mankind is to survive a move towards higher levels. . . . At present atomic energy is not a boon to mankind, but a menace.

It is an irony of fate that I, myself, have been the recipient of excessive admiration and respect from my fellows through no fault of my own.

My life is a simple thing that would interest no one. It is a known fact that I was born and that is all that is necessary.

There may be men who can live without political rights and without opportunity of free individual development, but I think this is intolerable for most Americans.

The discovery of nuclear chain reactions need not bring about the destruction of mankind any more than the discovery of matches.

When a man sits with a pretty girl for an hour, it seems like a minute. But let him sit on a hot stove for a minute—and it's longer than any hour. That's relativity.

Do you know that I am the only man in Princeton who never saw a football game?

DWIGHT DAVID EISENHOWER

✣ *This American general, a hero of World War II and the thirty-fourth President of the United States, was* born in 1890 at Denison, Texas.

When Dwight was one year old, his parents moved to Abilene, Kansas, where he attended the elementary grades and high school. His schoolmates predicted that he would end up as a professor of history at Yale, but this prediction proved false. Dwight *made* history instead of teaching it.

Homespun, friendly, unassuming, and congenial, he earned the nickname "Ike," which stuck to him as the most suitable for his character.

In 1915 he graduated from West Point, ranking 61st in a class of 168. His best subjects were engineering, military science, and drill.

During his distinguished military career, he was for four years on the staff of General MacArthur in the Philippines.

Early in World War II, he was made Commander in Chief of the Allied Forces in North Africa and later, in 1943, he became Supreme Commander of the Allied Expeditionary Forces in Europe. As such, he led the invasion of Normandy and, on May 7, 1945, received the surrender of the Germans at Rheims. Returning home, he was president of Columbia University from 1948 to 1952.

Eisenhower resigned from the Army in 1952. That same year he was elected President of the United States. Four years later, he was reelected for another term.

In politics, he called himself a "moderate." He favored the "free market system" instead of price and wage controls; he kept the Government out of labor disputes; he promoted missile programs and put an end to the Korean fighting. He was an ardent supporter of the United Nations.

Eisenhower led history's mightiest army to victory in World War II. Victor in war, he was a man of peace. He died in 1969.

. . . . .

Work should be for all of us a word as honorable and appealing as patriotism!

Every citizen must become involved, for on the current scene, apathy is scarcely less than a crime.

Abroad, in every major sector, we confront a formidable foe—and expansionist tyranny, which respects only toughness and strength and still displays little interest in peace, with honor and justice.

Remember, it is not by a tyrant's words, but only by his deeds that we can know him!

Strategy and tactics may change, there must never be any retreat from principle.

In spite of the publicity given to disorders, riots, and criminal violence, the vast portion of our people are law-abiding and proud of their country and ready to sacrifice on her behalf.

When you put on a uniform, there are certain inhibitions you accept.

(Asked if he had met General MacArthur:) I studied dramatics under him for five years in Washington and four years in the Philippines.

The true story of the war . . . is the story of a unity produced on the basis of . . . voluntary cooperation.

Only strength can cooperate. . . . Weakness . . . can only beg.

Next to the loss of freedom, war is the ultimate calamity which can befall a nation. . . . It is so horrible that imagination cannot grasp it in all its hideous aspects.

We merely want to live in peace with all the world, to trade with them, to commune with them, to learn from their culture as they may learn from ours . . . so that the products of our toil may be used for our schools and our roads and our churches and not for guns and planes and tanks and ships of war.

SIGMUND FREUD

✝ *He was the father of psychoanalysis, the science that penetrates the underground passages of the mind and* brings to the surface those long-forgotten impressions that determine behavior.

He believed that a complex of these repressed and forgotten impressions underlies all abnormal mental states, such as hysteria, and that merely revealing them to a patient can often effect a cure. He regarded the mental processes of childhood as particularly important to adult life. He developed the theory that dreams are the fulfillment of repressed desires.

Sigmund Freud was born of Jewish parents in 1856 in Freiberg, Moravia, now a part of Czechoslovakia, but he spent most of his life in Vienna, where he studied medicine at the University. Later he became a professor there.

Freud created an entirely new terminology in psychology —for example, *ambivalence*, which means the coexistence of opposing emotions; *compulsive*, used to describe repetitive acts caused by irresistible impulses; *ego*, the Latin word for *I*, which in the Freudian sense refers to the individual's conscious self; *id*, the wholly unconscious part of personality; *superego*, the part of the personality that embodies the latent conscience.

In 1938, already suffering from cancer, Freud had to flee before the onrushing Nazis. He found a refuge in England, but he died there in 1939.

· · · · ·

The truth cannot always be told openly, but somehow it does come out.

In general, one may distinguish two principal causes of name-forgetting: when the name itself touches something unpleasant, or when it is brought into connection with other associations which are influenced by such effects.

How far back into childhood do our memories reach? . . . Examinations show wide individual variations, inasmuch as some trace their first reminiscences to the sixth month of life, while others can recall nothing of their lives before the end of the sixth or even the eighth year.

Scenes of childhood: whether they prove true or false, one usually sees his own childish person both in contour and dress.

The dreams of little children are often simple fulfillments of wishes, and for this reason are, as compared with the dreams of adults, by no means interesting. They present no problem to be solved, but they are invaluable as affording proof that the dream, in its inmost essence, is the fulfillment of a wish.

This age of childhood, in which the sense of shame is unknown, seems a paradise when we look back upon it later, and paradise itself is nothing but the mass-phantasy of the childhood of the individual. This is why in paradise men are naked and unashamed, until the moment arrives when shame and fear awaken; expulsion follows, and sexual life and cultural development begin. Into this paradise dreams can take us back every night.

The forgetting of dreams, too, remains inexplicable until we seek to explain it by the power of the psychic censorship.

One overestimates the effect of child fears and of the terrifying stories told by nurses if one blames the latter for producing these fears in children. Children who are predisposed to fear absorb these stories which make no impression whatsoever upon others.

The forces which are destined to hold the sexual instinct in certain tracks are built up in infancy with the help of education.

Among the forces restraining the direction of the sexual instinct we have mentioned shame, loathing, sympathy, and the social constructions of morality and authority.

The dream serves preponderantly to guard against pain, while wit serves to acquire pleasure; in these two aims all our psychic activities meet.

Caricature, parody and travesty, like their practical counterpart unmasking, are directed against persons and objects who command authority and respect and who are exalted in some sense.

Taboos are very ancient prohibitions which at one time were forced upon a generation of primitive people from without, that is, they probably were forcibly impressed upon them by an earlier generation. These prohibitions concerned actions for which there existed a strong desire. The prohibitions maintained themselves from generation to generation, perhaps only as the result of a tradition set up by paternal and social authority.

ROBERT FROST

✣ *American poet, born in San Francisco in 1875. When he was ten, his father died, and he and his mother* returned to New England, the home of his ancestors. He was educated at Dartmouth and Harvard, but dropped in and out of school. When Frost married, his grandfather, who was disappointed in him, bought him a farm and said, "Go there and starve."

The Frosts and their children did not starve; they just barely had enough to eat. But the bucolic charm of rural New England made a poet out of Robert Frost. Four times he was awarded the Pulitzer Prize for poetry, and he became a professor of English at Amherst and a professor of poetry at Harvard.

President Kennedy was an admirer of Frost, and invited him to read a poem at the inauguration in 1961, when the poet was in his eighties. Frost replied, "If you can bear at your age the honor of being made President of the United States, I ought to be able at my age to bear the honor of taking some part in your inauguration. I may not be equal to it, but I can accept it for my cause—the arts, poetry, now for the first time taken into the affairs of statesmen."

On the platform, when he stepped forward to speak, the

glare from the sun and snow blinded him. He read three lines from a manuscript:

> *Summoning artists to participate*
> *In the august occasion of the state*
> *Seems something artists ought to celebrate.*

Frost stopped and said, "I am not having a good light here at all. I can't see in this light." Then from memory, he recited the poem "The Gift Outright"—*The land was ours before we were the land's.*

President Kennedy's favorite Frost poem was "Stopping by Woods on a Snowy Evening" and the line, *But I have promises to keep, and miles to go before I sleep.*

When Frost died in 1963, Kennedy flew to Amherst and paid a posthumous tribute to his favorite poet.

. . . . .

Good fences make good neighbors.

Home is the place where, when you have to go there, they have to take you in.

Pressed into service means pressed out of shape.

It is a coarse brutal world, unendurably coarse and brutal, for anyone who hasn't the least dash of coarseness or brutality in his own nature to enjoy it with.

No wonder poets sometimes have to seem so much more businesslike than business men. Their wares are so much harder to get rid of.

Nobody was ever meant to remember or invent what he did with every cent.

A jury consists of twelve persons chosen to decide who has the better lawyer.

By working faithfully eight hours a day, you may eventually get to be a boss and work twelve hours a day.

Half of the world is composed of people who have something to say and can't, and the other half who have nothing to say and keep on saying it.

I suppose I have been guided in life so far by instinct to protect what I was or wanted to be.

The world is full of willing people; some willing to work, the rest willing to let them.

Democracy is the best chance for the best people.

Earth's the right place for love.

JOHN KENNETH GALBRAITH

☆ | *This American economist, educator, and author does*
not consider himself an "ivory tower economist," but
one of the gladiators in the public arena of politics.

Galbraith was born on a farm at Jona Station, Ontario,
Canada, in 1908. He did his undergraduate work at the
University of Toronto, where he received a Bachelor of
Science degree, and then he studied at the University of
California at Berkeley. As an instructor and tutor at Har-
vard University, he had among his students John F.
Kennedy.

During World War II he became a director in the
Office of Price Administration, in charge of price control,
which was soon under attack for being excessive. Said
Galbraith, "I reached the point that all price-fixers reach—
my enemies outnumbered my friends."

When Kennedy became President, he sent his former
tutor as his Ambassador to India, "To do penance," he
said.

Galbraith is an unorthodox and challenging thinker, with
an acute sense of humor. Standing six feet eight inches,
he is one of the tallest men in American academic life. He
has written a number of books: *The Great Crash, 1929,*
American Capitalism, The Concept of Countervailing Pow-
er. His best known book is *The Affluent Society.*

. . . . .

Vietnam is not one issue. It's the whole issue.

If we were not in Vietnam, all that part of the world would be enjoying the obscurity it so richly deserves.

I am prepared to say that only one twentieth of one per-cent of the American people reads books carefully. But that's one hundred thousand people, and that's all I ever ask for. Some people think that they must write for two hundred million Americans. This is a terrible mistake.

If there are differences of opinion, there should be men to represent them.

I want to change things. I want to see things happen. I don't want just to talk about them.

The problem is those people who formed their ideas in the 1940's and the 1950's and have never changed them as the world has changed. . . . There is something wrong with people who make up their minds and don't change them.

MOHANDAS K. GANDHI

☥ | *The image is of a little man, dressed in a loincloth.*
He dedicated his life to Indian independence, and to
the peace and ennoblement of his people. He was called
Mahatma, the Great Soul, but he preferred to be called
Bapu, Father. He believed in the supreme force of nonviolence, of good will overcoming wrong intention. By
simple will, he taught, the weak can overpower the strong.

Gandhi was born in 1869, into a well-to-do Jain family.
The Jains are a puritanical branch of Hinduism, a sect
that keeps rigid rules of humanitarianism, vegetarianism,
charity, and abstinence. In accordance with the custom of
his caste, Gandhi was betrothed at eight and married at
thirteen. His wife bore him four sons. At eighteen, dressed
in Western clothes, Gandhi went to London to study.
After gaining his law degree, he returned to Bombay. When
he was twenty-three a law case took him to South Africa,
where he witnessed the oppression of Indians, who were
referred to there as "coolies." This changed his life. He
became the champion of the Indian cause. He inaugurated
his doctrine of civil disobedience, binding his followers to
disobey the law, but to endure unresistingly its penalties.

After twenty-one years in South Africa, Gandhi returned

to India to take up the battle for independence there. Because he felt that cotton from Yorkshire deprived his people of home industry, he began to spin his own yarn, urging his followers to do the same. The spinning wheel became a symbol of independence. Today it is pictured on the Indian flag.

At first, the Moslems cooperated with the Hindus in the fight for independence, but after many years, as the day of liberation neared, Moslem leaders began to clamor for a separate Moslem state, Pakistan. Gandhi was resolutely opposed to the division of India, but when the choice was between Moslem-Hindu warfare or the creation of Pakistan, Gandhi reluctantly and sadly agreed.

Indian Independence Day was August 15, 1947. On January 30, 1948, as Gandhi was walking through a garden in New Delhi on his way to address his daily prayer meeting, a Hindu fanatic fired at him three times. He died without ever regaining consciousness. His age at the time of his assassination was seventy-eight.

George Bernard Shaw summed it all up, "It shows how dangerous it is to be too good."

．　．　．　．　．

(When asked whether he was a politician or a saint:) I am a politician trying to be a saint.

I have regarded women as an incarnation of tolerance.

My shyness has been in reality my shield and buckler. It has allowed me to grow. It has helped me in my discernment of truth.

Prayers are no superstition; they act more real than the acts of eating, drinking, sitting, or walking.

Prayer needs no speech.

The woes of Mahatmas are known to Mahatmas alone.

I do not seek redemption from the consequences of my sin. I seek to be redeemed from sin itself, or rather from the very thought of sin.

It is the reformer who is anxious for the reform, and not society, from which he should expect nothing better than opposition, abhorrence, and even mortal persecution.

Golden shackles are far worse than iron ones.

Possession of arms implies an element of fear, if not of cowardice.

Bravery is not a quality of the body, it is of the soul.

Fear gone, there can be no hatred.

Let us fear God and we shall cease to fear man.

In matters of conscience, the law of majority has no place.

If by strength is meant moral power, then woman is immeasurably man's superior.

I hold that, the more helpless a creature, the more entitled it is to protection by man from the cruelty of man.

Democracy is not a state in which people act like sheep. Under democracy individual liberty of opinion and action are zealously guarded.

Fear has its use, but cowardice has none. I may not put my finger into the jaws of a snake, but the very sight of the snake need not strike terror into me.

Every duty performed confers upon one certain rights, whilst the exercise of every right carries with it certain obligations.

Anger is a sort of madness and the noblest causes have been damaged by advocates affected by temporary lunacy.

The highest form of freedom carries with it the greatest measure of discipline and humility. . . . Unbridled license is a sign of vulgarity, injurious alike to self and one's neighbors.

Students should have the greatest freedom of expression and of opinion. They may openly sympathize with any political party they like. But in my opinion, they may not have the freedom of action whilst they are studying. A student cannot be an active politician and pursue his studies at the same time.

CHARLES DE GAULLE

French soldier, the "Liberator" of France in World War II, and former President of the Republic, Charles de Gaulle is aloof, proud, highly cultivated, and a good writer.

Born in Lille in 1890, he was the son of a professor in a Jesuit school. During World War I he advocated a mechanized French army, and urged the construction of tanks and the training of men for tank corps. In 1940, during World War II, he was sent by Marshal Pétain to England to confer on military aid. When the French army collapsed, he refused to accept France's capitulation to Germany. He remained in England as head of the Free French National Committee, rallying Frenchmen to fight for the cause of a free France. For this he was court-martialed *in absentia* by the Pétain government and condemned to death.

But on V-E Day, Charles de Gaulle, at the head of the Free French forces, victoriously entered Paris.

President Roosevelt and Winston Churchill did not find him an easy ally during the war. Once Roosevelt said to Churchill, "He really thinks he's Joan of Arc." Churchill replied, "Yes, but the bishop won't let me burn him."

President Kennedy, on the other hand, was fascinated by

de Gaulle's role in history. He read his memoirs, and after their meeting in Paris he said, "I found General de Gaulle . . . a wise counselor for the future." But he shared the view that the General could be irritating, intransigent, insufferably vain, inconsistent, and impossible to please.

In spite of his differences with workers and students, the people of France consider de Gaulle one of the great Frenchmen of all time, and rightly so.

. . . . .

The positive side of my mind assures me that France is not actually herself unless she is in the front rank.

(He had imagined France as being:) Like a fairy princess or a madonna in a fresco, meant for eminent and exceptional fate . . . for accomplished success or exemplary misfortune.

France has lost a battle. But France has not lost the war.

Nothing enhances authority better than silence.

Without me, this country wouldn't be anything; without me, it would all have collapsed. For years, I've carried France on my shoulders.

I quarreled violently and bitterly with Churchill, but always got on with him. I never quarreled with Roosevelt, and never got on with him.

Pure English blood does not seem capable of producing a really strong man.

(Reply to a speaker who compared him to Robespierre:)
I always thought I was Jeanne d'Arc and Bonaparte. How
little one knows oneself.

How can you govern a country with 246 varieties of cheese?

DAG HAMMARSKJOLD

☩ *The man who was Secretary-General of the United Nations from April, 1953, to September, 1961, was* born in 1905 into a Swedish aristocratic family. His father, a conservative politician, was ambassador to Denmark, governor of a province and, during World War I, Prime Minister.

Throughout his school days Dag was an outstanding student. He applied himself to the study of law, economics, and French literature. At twenty-five he followed the example of his three elder brothers and entered civil service, where his rise was meteoric. When he was not yet thirty, he was undersecretary in the Treasury Department; at thirty-six he became chairman of the governors of the Bank of Sweden, and, subsequently, undersecretary in the Foreign Office. Twice he was a member of the Swedish delegation to the United Nations General Assembly, where he became known as a conscientious, unassuming civil servant. That was exactly the kind of man the great powers wanted for Secretary-General.

How badly they misjudged Hammarskjold's strength! Certainly he was self-effacing, preferring to work without fanfare, but he was one of the most progressive political thinkers of our time, leading the world organization boldly into new fields.

In 1956 he organized the first peace force in the Near East, to prevent clashes between Israelis and Arabs. In 1955 and 1958 he called two great international scientific conferences on the peaceful uses of atomic energy. Welcoming the newly independent nations of Africa and Asia to the UN, he saw to it they were provided with technical assistance, badly needed to help them toward self-sufficiency in the community of nations.

In July, 1960, when disorders broke out in the Congo, Hammarskjold set up an elaborate United Nations civilian and military operation to secure peace—and to prevent a local conflict from degenerating into a worldwide conflagration. It was in connection with this operation that he flew to the Congo in September, 1961. When his plane hit the treetops of the Ndola Forest, Dag Hammarskjold and fifteen others perished in the air crash.

After his death, his secret diary, *Markings*, was discovered in his New York apartment. The book is one more testimony that this "diplomat's diplomat" was guided by high moral and religious principles.

· · · · ·

To the diplomat of the middle of the twentieth century, war is something that must be averted at almost any cost.

It is when we all play safe that we create a world of the utmost insecurity.

The future will be all right because there will always be enough people to fight for a decent future.

Nationalism can serve as a stepping-stone toward international understanding. Is it not our childhood familiarity with the fields and the forest around our house which enables us to move with assurance on the soil of others?

Is it not on the basis of an insight into our mother tongue that we learn to speak other languages more easily?

It is possible to serve the world by serving our nations, and to serve our nations by serving the world.

Without recognition of human rights, we shall never have peace; and it is only within the framework of peace that human rights can be fully developed. In fact, the work for peace is basically a work for the most elementary human right: the right of everyone to security and freedom from fear.

It is for man to decide, whether outer space will be a new source of prosperity or a new source of holocaust.

Because it is more difficult to limit wars to a single area, all wars are of concern to all nations. Not only construction, but also destruction may today be global.

Never, "for the sake of peace and quiet," deny your own experience or convictions.

No nation or group of nations can base its future on a claim of supremacy. It is in its own interest that the other groups should have equal opportunities.

The weakness of one is the weakness of all, and the strength of one—not the military strength, but the real strength, the economic and social strength, the happiness of the people—is indirectly the strength of all.

The pursuit of peace and progress cannot end in a few years in either victory or defeat. The pursuit of peace and progress, with its trials and its errors, its successes and its setbacks, can never be relaxed and never abandoned.

The old is not so rotten, nor the new so immature, as many seem to think.

Conflicts, not only in human life, but also in the life of nations, are often never solved, but simply outgrown.

As individuals we know that the law which restrains us likewise protects us.

Dejection and despair lead to defeatism—and defeat.

There is a colonialism of the heart and of the mind, which no political decision can overcome and against which the battle must be waged within ourselves.

It is not the weak but the strong who practice tolerance, and the strong do not weaken their position showing tolerance.

Man must master his world, but in order to do so, he must
know it.

The effort to realize, by honest agreement on earth, peace
and good will toward men is worthy of the greatest sacrifice
a true man can bring.

HERMANN HESSE

☿ | *German poet and novelist, born in 1877 in the little*
♈ | *Swabian town of Calw, Würtemberg. His parents were*
Pietist missionaries in India. Brought back to Europe by
ill health, his father became editor of a magazine, and
director of a Pietist publishing house.

Hermann, a lively, sensitive, headstrong youngster, was
the despair of his teachers. He deserted school to become an
apprentice in a bookstore, a manual laborer, helper in his
father's publishing house, and salesman in a bookstore in
the university town of Tubingen. His literary career began
there, when he published his first volume of verses and
romantic prose.

In 1899 he moved to Basel, Switzerland. In 1904 he married for the first time, but in 1911 his restless soul drove
him toward the Orient—Ceylon, Malaya, Sumatra—and he
reported on his travels in diarylike writings.

Hesse was a prolific writer. In his novels, he chastised the
twentieth century as a materialistic age in which man has
lost his soul to machines, money, and physical comfort, and
can no longer appreciate beauty and artistic creation. Medi-
ocrity rules the world, and the sensitive worshipers of
beauty, the seekers of truth and of the deeper meaning of
life, are considered misfits.

Hesse was a lean, lonely man. His work was inspired by the romantic mysticism of the Orient, and has the mood of a dream. Among his writings are *Steppenwolf, Narcissus and Goldmund, Siddhartha,* and *Magister Ludi.* He was awarded the Nobel Prize in 1946. He died in 1962.

. . . . .

Solitude is independence.

The man of power is ruined by power, the man of money by money, the submissive man by subservience, the pleasure seeker by pleasure.

The bourgeois today burns as heretics and hangs as criminals those to whom he erects monuments tomorrow.

He who sentimentally sings of blessed childhood is thinking of the return to nature and innocence and the origin of things, and has quite forgotten that these blessed children are beset with conflict and complexities and capable of all suffering.

Obeying is like eating and drinking. There's nothing like it if you've been without it too long.

The saints, these are the true men, the younger brothers of the Savior.

The modern man . . . has lost the love of inanimate objects. He does not even love his most sacred object, his motorcar, but is ever hoping to change it as soon as he can for a later model.

True humor begins when a man ceases to take himself seriously.

It is open to a man to give himself up wholly to spiritual views, to seeking after God, to the ideal of saintliness. On the other hand, he can equally give himself up entirely to the life of instinct, to the lusts of the flesh, and so direct all his efforts to the attainment of momentary pleasures. The one path leads to the saint, to the martyrdom of the spirit and surrender to God. The other path leads to the profligate, to the martyrdom of the flesh, the surrender to corruption.

For it appears to be an inborn and imperative need of all men to regard the self as a unit.

As a body everyone is single, as a soul never.

The next war . . . draws nearer and nearer, and it will be a good deal more horrible than the last.

Life is no poem of heroism with heroic parts to play and so on, but a comfortable room where people are quite content with eating and drinking, coffee and knitting, cards and wireless.

Animals' eyes are always serious.

Many persons pass for normal, and indeed for highly valuable members of society, who are incurably mad; and many, on the other hand, are looked upon as mad who are geniuses.

Now and again I have expressed the opinion that every nation, and even every person, would do better, instead of rocking himself to sleep with political catchwords about war and guilt, to ask himself how far his own faults and negligences and evil tendencies are guilty of the war and all the other wrongs of the world, and that therein lies the only possible means of avoiding the next war.

Man is an onion made up of a hundred integuments, a texture made up of many threads.

Man is not by any means of fixed and enduring form. . . . He is nothing else than the narrow and perilous bridge between nature and spirit.

My nature had much of the child in it, its curiosity and love for idleness and play. Well, and so it went on and on, till I saw that sooner or later there must be enough of play.

Well, look at an animal, a cat, a dog, or a bird, or one of those beautiful great beasts in the zoo, a puma or a giraffe. You can't help seeing that all of them are right. They're never in any embarrassment. They always know what to do and how to behave themselves. They don't flatter and they don't intrude. They don't pretend. They are as they are, like stones or flowers or stars in the sky. Don't you agree?

POPE JOHN XXIII

John XXIII brought to the Holy See a warmth and humanity that won him the affection of people of all nationalities and faiths. It was not without reason that some people irreverently nicknamed him John the Jolly.

Pope John was a stout man, and sometimes he liked to make fun of himself. Once he was visited by a very skinny man, and he said, "We will both have to say a prayer to God, beseeching Him to remove half the excess fat which I have and to give it to you."

He was born Angelo Giuseppe Roncalli, in 1881, in a little village in Lombardy, Italy. His father and his brothers were small peasant farmers. He always remembered with pride being the son of "a humble but robust and honest laborer." In World War I he served as a sergeant in the Italian army.

He was Patriarch of Venice when, at the age of seventy-eight, he was elected Pope. Soon tales began to circulate about his kindness, simplicity, and geniality—how he had offered a glass of wine to his gardener, how he had visited on Christmas Day the inmates of a prison, and how he broke the custom by which a Pope always eats alone and invited his peasant brothers or a friend to lunch with him.

After lunch he even smoked a cigarette!

If some had expected that this aged man would prove to be only a stop-gap pope, the belief rapidly proved false. Pope John led the Church into new directions. He showed his deep concern for the problems of all people, advocating international social justice, not only for Catholics but for men of every creed, color, and ideology. He named new cardinals and bishops of all races. In 1962 he called together the Second Vatican Council to advise him. It is noteworthy that when the First Vatican Council opened in 1869 it was attended by 744 bishops, most of whom were European. To the Second Council came 2540 bishops from every corner of the earth and from many races. Little more than a third of them were from Europe.

John XXIII died in 1963. He had the wisdom of a ruler, the humility of a saint, and the lightheartedness of the eternal child. Whatever popes may come after him there can hardly be another who will fill his place in the hearts of his fellowmen.

. . . . .

(A twelve-year-old boy wrote him a letter. "My dear Pope: I am undecided. I want to be a policeman or a pope. What do you think?") If you want my opinion, learn how to be a policeman, because that cannot be improvised. As regards being Pope . . . anybody can be Pope; the proof of this is that I have become one.

Naturalness is found in simplicity, and divinity in naturalness.

We must always try to speak to the good in people. Nothing can be lost by trying. Everything can be lost if men do not find some way to work together to save the peace. I am not afraid to talk to anyone about peace on earth.

The solidarity of the human race and Christian brotherhood demand the elimination as far as possible of . . . discrepancies. . . . This solidarity which binds all men together as members of a common family makes it impossible for wealthy nations to look with indifference upon the hunger, misery, and poverty of other nations, whose citizens are unable to enjoy even elementary human rights.

If God created shadows it was in order to better emphasize the light.

There are no political communities which are superior by nature, and none which are inferior.

It is in keeping with their dignity as persons that human beings should take an active part in government.

Every human being has the right to honor God according to the dictates of an upright conscience.

It is impossible to determine, once and for all, what is the most suitable form of government.

No political community is able to pursue its own interests and develop itself in isolation. Today the universal common good poses problems of worldwide dimensions, which cannot be adequately tackled or solved except on a worldwide basis.

It is our earnest wish that the United Nations organization —in its structure and in its means—may become ever more equal to the magnitude and nobility of its tasks.

The person who errs is always and above all a human being, and he retains in every case his dignity as a human person, and he must be always regarded and treated in accordance with that lofty dignity.

It must be borne in mind that to proceed gradually is the law of life in all its expressions, therefore in human institutions too, it is not possible to renovate for the better except by working from within them gradually.

Justice . . . right, reason, and humanity urgently demand that the arms race should cease. That stockpiles which exist in various countries should be reduced equally and simultaneously by the parties concerned. That nuclear weapons should be banned.

The true and solid peace of nations consists not in equality of arms, but in mutual trust alone.

The talk of war is still serious. It will be a slaughter which will end in a universal act of expiation. But oh, what sorrow for so many mothers, wives, and innocent creatures.

Calm of spirit in the face of difficulties constitutes my strength.

There has been talk of a political pope, of a scholarly pope, of a diplomatic pope, when the Pope is just the Pope. He is the good shepherd who seeks to reach souls and to look upon the truth. Truth and goodness are like two wings. We must not fashion a pope according to our plans.

(In an address to Romans:) When you go back to your homes, hug your children for me. Tell them that is an affectionate embrace from the Pope!

Peace is the house of all.

CARL GUSTAV JUNG

☨ | *Carl Gustav Jung, the son of an Evangelical minister,*
| *was born in 1875, in Kesswil, Switzerland.* The family
moved to Basel, where he obtained a medical degree at the
University of Basel in 1900. After additional studies in
Paris, Dr. Jung became a lecturer in psychiatry at the University of Zurich.

A pioneer in analytic psychology, he worked with Sigmund Freud in Vienna. Later he broke with Freud, who
held that nearly all mental troubles were the result of sexual
conflicts in infancy. Dr. Jung admitted the validity of
Freud's views, but believed that man's religious instinct was
perhaps as strong as his sexual instinct.

Another difference between him and Freud was Freud's
method of placing his subject on a couch during psychoanalysis. Jung usually placed his subject in a chair opposite
him.

In 1911 Dr. Jung, with others, founded the International
Psychoanalytic Society to further his views on new elements
that he believed he had found in dreams and phantasies.
He also explored yoga, alchemy, folklore, and obscure tribal
religious rites and taboos.

His opponents considered all this a waste of time, but

Jung said that these elements were in man's mind, and if you wanted to understand man's mind, you had to know what it contained. He created such terms as *extrovert*—outward looking, and *introvert*—inward looking, soul searching. He derided the Freudian theory that God was nothing more than man's self-created vision of his father. Jung held that man had a storehouse of collective experiences tucked away deep in his mind, including a never-ceasing urge toward religion.

Therefore it is not surprising that among Jung's interests was the study of flying saucers. He believed they represented a new "savior myth."

In 1945 Dr. Jung gave up his professorship at the University of Basel to concentrate on his research and his writing. During that time he lived at Lake Lucerne and rested in an old stone tower near Bollingen. It was Bollingen that gave the name to the series of his books published in the United States.

He died in 1961 at the age of eighty-five.

．　．　．　．　．

Great gifts are the fairest, and often the most dangerous, fruits on the tree of humanity. They hang on the weakest branches, which easily break.

Sometimes, indeed, there is such a discrepancy between the genius and his human qualities that one has to ask oneself whether a little less talent might not have been better.

Creative powers can just as easily turn out to be destructive. It rests solely with the moral personality whether they apply themselves to good things or to bad. And if this is lacking, no teacher can supply it or take its place.

The gifted child will do well to accustom himself early to the fact that any excellence puts him in an exceptional position and exposes him to a great many risks, the chief of which is an exaggerated self-confidence. Against this the only protection is humility and obedience, and even these do not always work.

School comrades take the place of brothers and sisters; the teacher, if a man, acts as a substitute for the father, and, if a woman, for the mother.

(About flying saucers:) I can only say for certain that the things are not a mere rumor, something has been seen. A purely psychological explanation is ruled out.

Life is not made up of yesterdays only.

I could not say I believe. I know! I have had the experience of being gripped by something that is stronger than myself, something that people call God.

I have treated many hundreds of patients. . . . Among [those] in the second half of life—that is to say, over 35— there has not been one whose problem in the last resort was not that of finding a religious outlook on life.

Individuation means to become what one is really meant to be. In Zen Buddhism they have a saying: "Show your natural face." I think I have shown my natural face, often to the bewilderment of my time.

An understanding heart is everything in a teacher, and cannot be esteemed highly enough. One looks back with appreciation to the brilliant teachers, but with gratitude to those who touched our human feelings. The curriculum is so much necessary raw material, but warmth is the vital element for the growing plant and for the soul of the child.

Mathematics presupposes a definite mental aptitude which by no means everybody possesses and which cannot be acquired. For those who do not possess it, mathematics can only be learnt by rote like a jumble of meaningless words. Such persons may be highly gifted in every other way, and may possess the capacity for logical thinking already, or can acquire it more easily through direct instruction in logic.

JOHN F. KENNEDY

♏ | *John Fitzgerald Kennedy was born in 1917, the second*
♈ | *son in a family of nine children.* His father was a
businessman who became United States Ambassador to
Great Britain; his mother, Rose Fitzgerald, was the daughter of a Boston politician. The Kennedys were "Irish-Amer-
icans," the descendants of people who had immigrated to
America in a time of great hardship—the potato famine of
1850.

Jack majored in political science at Harvard, and he graduated *cum laude.* For a while he traveled in Europe. Then
World War II broke out, and he volunteered, joining the
Navy. In 1943 he was in command of a torpedo boat that
was rammed by a Japanese destroyer and cut in two. Although hurt, Jack managed to save the life of a wounded
comrade by taking the strap of his life preserver between
clenched teeth and towing him, for five hours, to the nearest
island.

Back home, he entered politics. In 1947, at the age of
twenty-nine, he became a congressman. Five years later he
was United States Senator from Massachusetts. In 1960 he
was elected the thirty-fifth president of the United States.
He was the first American president to be born in the

twentieth century, and was the youngest man and the first Catholic ever to hold such a high office in this country.

During his thousand days in the White House, he opened new frontiers to his country. He established the Peace Corps, through which young volunteers go to the under-developed countries and help people to help themselves. He inaugurated the Alliance for Progress, to give economic aid to Latin-American countries. He championed the new nations in Africa. He supported the space exploration program, and it was during his term that Colonel John H. Glenn, Jr., made the first successful orbital flight. He proposed the most sweeping civil rights legislation in history, to give all Americans equal opportunity in education, employment, and housing. He signed the Nuclear Test Ban Treaty, and with great tact and a firm hand he improved United States relations with the Soviet Union.

He was an excellent writer and an articulate speaker, a witty, humane, and dedicated man. During his term of office, the White House became the meeting place of great musicians, writers, and men of science.

In 1963, this most remarkable president was assassinated in Dallas, Texas, leaving the entire nation—in fact, people all over the world—in profound sadness.

. . . . .

Let the word go forth from this time and place, to friend and foe alike, that the torch has been passed to a new generation of Americans.

Let every nation know, whether it wishes us well or ill, that we shall pay any price, bear any burden, meet any hardship, support any friend, oppose any foe to assure the survival of the success of liberty.

My country intends to be a participant and not merely an observer in the peaceful, expeditious movement of nations from the status of colonies to the partnership of equals.

Man's unsatisfied aspirations for economic progress and social justice can best be achieved by free men working within a framework of democratic institutions.

The name "America" was given to this continent by a *German* mapmaker, Martin Waldseemuller, to honor an *Italian* explorer, Amerigo Vespucci. The three ships which discovered America sailed under *Spanish* flag, were commanded by an *Italian* sea captain, and included in their crew an *Englishman*, a *Jew*, and a *Negro*.

We cannot speak of a particular "immigrant's contribution" to America because all Americans have been immigrants or the descendants of immigrants.

One hundred years of delay have passed since President Lincoln freed the slaves, yet their heirs, their grandsons, are not fully free. They are not yet freed from the bonds of injustice. They are not yet freed from social and economic oppression. And this nation, for all its hopes and all its boasts, will not be fully free until all its citizens are free.

Those who make peaceful revolution impossible will make violent revolution inevitable.

Art is the great democrat, calling forth creative genius from every sector of society, disregarding race or religion or wealth or color.

The quality of American life must keep pace with the quantity of American goods. This country cannot afford to be materially rich and spiritually poor.

A man may die, nations may rise and fall, but an idea lives on. Ideas have endurance without death.

Those who came before us made certain that this country rode the first waves of the industrial revolution, the first waves of modern invention and the first wave of nuclear power. And this generation does not intend to flounder in the backwash of the coming age of space. We mean to be part of it. We mean to lead it, for the eyes of the world now look into space, to the moon and to the planets beyond; and we have vowed that we shall not see it governed by a hostile flag of conquest, but by the banner of freedom and peace. We have vowed that we shall not see space filled with weapons of mass destruction, but with instruments of knowledge and understanding.

I would say to the leaders of the Soviet Union and to their people that if either of our countries is to be fully secure, we need a much better weapon than the H-bomb, a weapon better than ballistic missiles or nuclear submarines—and that better weapon is peaceful cooperation.

The basic problems facing the world today are not susceptible to a military solution.

It did not matter who fired first or was annihilated last.

We have the power to make this the best generation of mankind in the history of the world—or to make it the last.

But peace does not rest in the charters and covenants alone. It lies in the hearts and minds of all people. . . . So let us not rest all our hopes on parchment and on paper, let us strive to build peace, a desire for peace, a willingness to work for peace in the heart and mind of all of our people. I believe that we can. I believe the problems of human destiny are not beyond the reach of human beings.

The decision is ours. Never have the nations of the world had so much to lose, or so much to gain. Together we shall save our planet—or together we shall perish in its flames. Save it we can, and save it we must, and then shall we earn the eternal thanks of mankind and, as peacemakers, the eternal blessing of God.

All this will not be finished in the first one hundred days. Nor will it be finished in the first one thousand days, nor in the life of this administration, nor even perhaps in our lifetime on this planet. But let us begin. . . .

Our children and our grandchildren are not merely statistics towards which we can be indifferent.

Children are the world's most valuable resource and its best hope for the future.

I realize that the pursuit of peace is not as dramatic as the pursuit of war—and frequently the words of the pursuer fall on deaf ears. But we have no more urgent task. . . .

Our problems are man made, therefore they can be solved by man. And man can be as big as he wants.

What kind of peace do I mean? What kind of peace do we seek? Not a *Pax Americana* enforced on the world by American weapons of war. Not the peace of the grave or the security of the slave. I am talking about a genuine peace, the kind of peace that makes life on earth worth living, the kind that enables men and nations to grow and to hope and to build a better life for their children—not merely peace for Americans, but peace for all men and women; not merely peace in our time, but peace for all time.

We prefer world law in the age of self-determination, to world war in the age of mass extermination. . . . Every man, woman, and child lives under a nuclear sword of Damocles, hanging by the slenderest of threads, capable of being cut at any moment by accident or miscalculation or by madness. The weapons of war must be abolished before they abolish us.

Let us never negotiate out of fear, but let us never fear to negotiate.

And so, my fellow Americans: ask not what your country can do for you—ask what you can do for your country.

My fellow citizens of the world: ask not what America will do for you, but what together we can do for the freedom of man.

In the long history of the world, only a few generations have been granted the role of defending freedom in its hour of maximum danger. I do not shrink from this responsibility— I welcome it. I do not believe that any of us would exchange places with any other people or any other generation. The energy, the faith, the devotion which we bring to this endeavor will light our country and all who serve it—and the glow from that fire can truly light the world.

NIKITA SERGEIEVITCH KHRUSHCHEV

This Soviet leader and premier was born in 1894. The son of a miner, in a poverty-stricken village near Kursk, he had no formal schooling. He worked as shepherd boy, pipe fitter, and locksmith. In 1918 he joined the Bolsheviks and fought in the Civil War. After the war he took up mining and went to night school. In 1929 he entered Moscow's Industrial Academy and began his Communist Party activities in earnest. His star rose as Stalin liquidated his former friends, and their places became vacant. After Stalin's death, it was Khrushchev who liquidated Stalin's remaining friends by sending them to Outer Mongolia.

By 1956 he was the almighty boss of the Soviet Union. In one three-hour indictment he demolished the image of his former protector, Stalin, calling him "murderer" and "maniac." In 1960 Mr. Khrushchev came to New York to the United Nations General Assembly meeting. He is remembered for banging on his desk with two fists and taking off his shoes. He did his best to impress the new African members of the UN—but he did it the wrong way. His unusual behavior contributed to his downfall in 1964, when he was judged guilty of "boasting, phrase mongering, and hare-brained ideas."

Once ousted, he became an "un-person." His name was erased from the Soviet Encyclopedia; his pictures were taken off the walls. He became just a little old man sitting in his garden, his dog and a portable radio at his side.

. . . . .

No matter how humble a man's beginning, he achieves the stature of the office to which he is elected.

If you cannot catch the bird of paradise better take a wet hen.

Life is short. Live it up. See all you can. Hear all you can and go all you can.

To me it makes no difference whether I am involved in the explosion of a "clean" or a "dirty" atomic bomb because both would kill me.

You may call me a pot but don't put me on a stove.

It is not wrong to throw in a piece of bacon and a piece of butter in the course of improving the theory of Marx.

If you didn't give a turkey a passport, you couldn't tell the difference between a Communist and Capitalist turkey.

Who is certain? Only a fool is completely certain. Only a fool thinks he knows everything and only a fool is completely happy. For the more one learns the more one learns how much there is yet to know.

Bureaucrats sprout like mushrooms after a rainfall.

If I tell my Foreign Minister to sit on a block of ice and stay there for months, he will do it without backtalk.

Trust God and look out for yourself. When you walk among dogs, don't forget to carry a stick. After all, that is what a hound has teeth for, to bite when he feels like it.

If anyone tries to interfere in our affairs, if you will excuse the rather indelicate phrase, we will just give them a punch in the nose.

(To Western diplomats:) We will bury you.

In our time, when rocket developments are rapid, no distance will protect any country from the effects of atomic and hydrogen weapons.

"Comrade Khrushchev," Mao said, "you have only to provoke the Americans to military action and I will give you as many people as you wish—one hundred divisions, two hundred divisions, a thousand." With contemporary techniques, his divisions meant nothing, because one or two rockets would be enough to turn all the divisions to dust.

It is much better to live in peace than to live with loaded pistols.

Let's compete, let's coexist peacefully, even if it's without love and by necessity, but coexist we must since Capitalist and Socialist countries are on one planet.

Just now I was told that I could not go to Disneyland. I asked, "Why not? What is it? Do you have rocket launching pads there? I do not know. . . . Is there an epidemic of cholera there or something? Or have gangsters taken hold of the place that can destroy me? Then what must I do? Commit suicide?" That is the situation—I am your guest. For me the situation is inconceivable. I cannot find words to explain this to my people.

History is not a horse, it cannot be driven with a whip.

MARTIN LUTHER KING, JR.

✣ | *Born in 1929 into a middle-class Negro family whose*
  | *members had been active for two generations in the*
civil rights cause, he was named Michael after his father,
pastor of Ebenezer Baptist Church in Atlanta, Georgia.
Michael was five when his father changed both their names
to Martin, in honor of the leader of the Reformation,
Martin Luther.

Following in his father's footsteps, Martin, Jr., prepared
for the ministry. As a student at Crozer Theological Seminary in Chester, Pennsylvania, he discovered the writings
of Mohandas Gandhi, the Hindu leader, whose mystic faith
in nonviolent protest became his inspiration.

Moving on to Boston University, King gained his doc-
torate and met his future wife, Coretta Scott.

In 1954 Dr. King took his first pastorate, in Montgomery,
Alabama. He formed the Southern Christian Leadership
Conference and helped to form the Students Nonviolent
Coordinating Committee. His entire life was now conse-
crated to the perilous fight for the freedom of the Negro
people in America. He wrote: "I have known very few quiet
days in the past years. I have been imprisoned in Alabama
and Georgia jails twelve times. My home has been bombed

twice. I have been the victim of a near-fatal stabbing. At times I have felt that I could no longer bear such a heavy burden, and have been tempted to retreat to a more serene life. But every time that temptation appeared, something came to strengthen and sustain my determination. I have learned now that the Master's burden is light precisely when we take his yoke upon us."

Dr. Martin Luther King, Jr., once told his congregation what he wanted for a eulogy. "Now and then," he said, "I think about my own death and I think about my own funeral. And I don't think about it in a morbid sense. And every now and then I ask myself what it is that I would want said, and I leave the word to you this morning.

"If any of you are around when I have to meet my day I don't want a long funeral.

"And if you get somebody to deliver the eulogy tell him not to talk too long.

"And every now and then I wonder what I want him to say.

"Tell him not to mention that I have a Nobel Peace Prize—that isn't important.

"Tell him not to mention that I have three hundred or four hundred other awards—that's not important. Tell him not to mention where I went to school.

"I'd like somebody to mention that day that Martin Luther King, Jr., tried to give his life serving others.

"I'd like for somebody to say that day that Martin Luther King, Jr., tried to love somebody.

"I want you to say that day that I tried to be right and to walk with them. I want you to be able to say that day that I did try to feed the hungry. I want you to be able to say that day that I did try in my life to clothe the naked. I want you to say on that day that I did try in my life to visit those who were in prison. And I want you to say that I tried to love and serve humanity.

"Yes, if you want to, say that I was a drum major. Say that I was a drum major for justice. Say that I was a drum major for peace. I was a drum major for righteousness.

"And all of the other shallow things will not matter.

"I won't have any money to leave behind. I won't have the fine and luxurious things of life to leave behind. But I just want to leave a committed life behind.

"And that is all I want to say. If I can help somebody as I pass along, if I can cheer somebody with a well song, if I can show somebody he's traveling wrong, then my living will not be in vain.

"If I can do my duty as a Christian ought. If I can bring salvation to a world once wrought.

"If I can spread my message as the Master taught.

"Then my living will not be in vain."

．　．　．　．　．

I refuse to accept the view that mankind is so tragically bound to the starless midnight of racism and war that the bright daybreak of peace and brotherhood can never become a reality.

We will win our freedom because the sacred heritage of our nation and the eternal will of God are embodied in our echoing demands.

I have a dream that one day this nation will rise up and

live out the true meaning of its creed . . . that all men are created equal. I have a dream that one day even the state of Mississippi, a state sweltering with the heat of oppression, will be transformed into an oasis of freedom and justice. I have a dream that my four little children will one day live in a nation where they will not be judged by the color of their skin but by the content of their character. I have a dream today, and if America is to be a great nation, this must become true.

Black Power is an often implicit and often explicit belief in black separatism. . . . Few ideas are more unrealistic. There is no salvation for the Negro through isolation.

Hate is always tragic. It is as injurious to the hater as it is to the hated. It distorts the personality and scars the soul. . . . As a race we must work passionately and unrelentingly for first-class citizenship, but we must never use second-class methods to gain it.

I am still convinced that nonviolence is both the most practically sound and morally excellent way to grapple with the age-old problem of racial injustice.

We must learn to live together as brothers or we will perish together as fools. . . .Racial injustice is still the black man's burden and the white man's shame. . . . The government must certainly share the guilt, the individual must share the guilt, and even the church must share the guilt.

America, you have strayed away, you have trampled over

nineteen million of your brethren. All men are created equal. Not some men. Not white men. All men. America, rise up and come home.

The quality, not the longevity, of one's life is what is important.

Before I will be a slave, I will be dead in my grave.

We will match your capacity to inflict suffering with our capacity to endure suffering. We will meet your physical force with soul force. We will not hate you, but we cannot in all good conscience obey your unjust laws. We will soon wear you down by our capacity to suffer. And in winning our freedom we will so appeal to your heart and conscience that we will win you in the process.

So listen to me, children: put on your marching shoes: don'cha get weary; though the path ahead may be dark and dreary; we're walking for freedom, children.

In the spirit of the darkness of this hour, we must not despair, we must not become bitter—we must not lose faith in our white brothers.

The question is not whether we will be extremist but what kind of extremist we will be. Will we be extremists for hate or will we be extremists for love? Will we be extremists for the preservation of injustice—or will we be extremists for the cause of justice?

Some of you have knives, and I ask you to put them up.

Some of you have arms, and I ask you to put them up. Get the weapon of nonviolence, the breastplate of righteousness, the armor of truth, and just keep marching.

I believe that unarmed truth and unconditional love will have the final word in reality. That is why right, temporarily defeated, is stronger than evil triumphant.

(On April 4, 1968, in the evening, Martin Luther King, Jr., was killed by a white gunman in a Memphis motel. The day before his murder, on April 3, 1968, as if by premonition, he made the following statement in a speech:)

We've got some difficult days ahead. But it really doesn't matter with me now. Because I've been to the mountaintop, I won't mind. Like anybody, I would like to live a long life. Longevity has its place. But I'm not concerned about that now. I just want to do God's will. And He's allowed me to go up to the mountain. And I've looked over, and I've seen the Promised Land. I may not get there with you, but I want you to know tonight that we as a people will get to the Promised Land. So I'm happy tonight. I'm not fearing any man. Mine eyes have seen the glory of the coming of the Lord.

LIN YUTANG

This Chinese author and philologist was born at Changchow, Amoy, in 1895. He was educated at St. John's University in Shanghai, and later studied at Harvard and at Leipzig in Germany. From 1923 to 1926, he was professor of English philology at the University of Peking.

Lin Yutang is a witty and wise writer. One of his best known works is *My Country and My People*. Since the time of its writing, China has become Communist, yet the book contains so many deep human observations that it remains instructive, meaningful, and delightful reading today.

Good books just never grow old.

. . . . .

The dog which remembers only to bark and not to bite, and is led through the streets as a lady's pet, is only a degenerate wolf.

The real question of physical and moral health in man as well as in animals is how well he is able to do his work and enjoy his life, and how fit he is yet to survive.

When one cannot be powerful, one must choose to be

dainty, and when one cannot be aggressive, one has to make a virtue of reasonableness.

The standard that measures a man's civilization by the number of mechanical buttons he presses in a day must . . . be a false standard.

Only ideas that come straight from man's heart will survive.

Poetry is essentially thoughts colored with emotion.

No amount of money can make an uncreative mind tell a good story.

We do not know a man until we know how he spends his leisure.

People move into a three-room flat then wonder why they can never keep their children home.

Responsibility makes men sober, and a national cultural tradition helps them to think sanely about life.

Of all the rights of women, the greatest is to be a mother.

Women have a surer instinct of life than men. . . . Many women believe a thing is so because it is so.

Common sense and the practical mind are characteristics of women rather than of men, who are more liable to take their feet off the ground and soar to impossible heights.

In times of any emergency, I always depend on the judgment of a woman rather than that of a man.

A simple but hearty meal eaten without much worry is . . . a great deal of luck.

Preachers should not be afraid to condemn a bad steak from their pulpits.

There is a Chinese saying that it is better to be a dog in peaceful times than be a man in times of unrest.

Pacifism is not "noble"; it is simply "good" because it is common sense.

MAO TSE-TUNG

Chinese political leader, one of the founders of the Chinese Communist Party.

He was born in 1893, in Hunan province in Central China, son of an impoverished peasant family. He always hated his father.

He prepared to become a grammar-school teacher. As he neared graduation, Mao advertised for friends in a local newspaper under the pseudonym of "the fellow with twenty-eight strikes"—Mao Tse-tung being written in Chinese with twenty-eight strokes of the brush.

He eventually went to Peking to become assistant to the university librarian. Mao began to read radical books, and in 1921 he was invited to attend the first meeting of the Chinese Communist Party in Shanghai.

Before he rose to power in the party, he was expelled three times from the Central Committee and received eight warnings. When the Japanese invaded Manchuria in 1931, he joined forces with the moderate Chinese party to fight the invaders. In 1937, when the war was over, he tried his hand as a Communist guerrilla fighter, organizing the peasants.

In World War II he was again on the side of the angels,

but soon he was fighting both the Japanese and the Chinese Nationalists. After World War II he emerged as the Communist boss of China.

A close collaborator described him as physically weak—he had to be assisted in mounting his horse.

He is a chain smoker, keeps a flask of wine on his desk, and suffers from insomnia. While he can be rude in getting rid of his opposition, he writes tender poetry, and he is proud of his poems for he sometimes gives autographed copies to his friends.

As a fat man he can swim seven miles; to be exact, he floats seven miles on the water.

He follows an expansionist policy. He occupied Tibet. From time to time he wages war against India's northern provinces. He actively participated in the Korean War, on the side of North Korea, and is a staunch supporter of North Vietnam.

He sees two enemies: the United States and the Soviet Union. He developed the hydrogen bomb and boasted to Yugoslavia's Marshal Tito that in an atomic war China would emerge victorious. "Even if three hundred million Chinese were killed, there would still remain another three hundred million," he said. He didn't mention that the leftovers would be maimed by radiation.

Communist China, not being a "peace-loving" nation, is not seated at the United Nations, because an insufficient number of member nations will agree to it.

.   .   .   .   .

A revolution is not a dinner party, or writing an essay, or painting a picture, or doing embroidery; it cannot be so refined, so leisurely and gentle, so temperate, kind, courteous, restrained, and magnanimous. A revolution is an insurrection, an act of violence by which one class overthrows another.

"War is the continuation of politics." In this sense war is politics and war itself is a political action; since ancient times there has never been a war that did not have a political character.

It can therefore be said that politics is war without bloodshed while war is politics with bloodshed.

Every Communist must grasp the truth, "Political power grows out of the barrel of a gun."

Yes, we are advocates of the omnipotence of revolutionary war; that is good, not bad; it is Marxist. The guns of the Russian Communist Party created socialism.

War can only be abolished through war, and in order to get rid of the gun it is necessary to take up the gun.

To the present day, all weapons are still an extension of the spear and the shield.

The tank is a new weapon combining the functions of both spear and shield.

Sacrifice and self-preservation are both opposite and complementary to each other.

Be a pupil before you become a teacher.

Learn to "play the piano." In playing the piano all ten fingers are in motion; it won't do to move some fingers only and not others. But if all ten fingers press down at once, there is no melody.

To produce good music, the ten fingers should move rhythmically and in coordination.

The atom bomb is a paper tiger which the U. S. reactionaries use to scare people. It looks terrible, but in fact it isn't.

As for the training courses, the main objective should still be to raise the level of technique in marksmanship, bayoneting, grenade-throwing and the like, and the secondary objective should be to raise the level of tactics, while special emphasis should be laid on night operations.

A frog in a well says, "The sky is no bigger than the mouth of the well."

TOM MBOYA

Tom Mboya was an African labor leader from Kenya, a leading spokesman for the Pan-African movement. He was born in 1930. His parents were illiterate workers on a sisal plantation.

Between 1942 and 1948 he attended a Roman Catholic school. Later he entered a training school for sanitary inspectors. In 1951 he got an inspector's job in Nairobi.

In 1952 Mboya joined the Kenya African Union, and the next year he was chosen general secretary of the Kenya Federation of Labor. In those days Tom Mboya often visited the United States, and he was received by Richard Nixon, who was then Vice-President.

Active in the leadership of the anti-Communist International Confederation of Free Trade Unions, he disavowed violence. Mboya was the youngest member of the fifty-man delegation sent to the London conference that worked out the details of Kenyan independence, which came in 1963. Afterward he became Minister of Economic Planning and Development.

In July, 1969, his career was cut short by an assassin's bullet in a crowded Nairobi street.

· · · · ·

When we left for London, the government was in the hands of the Europeans. Now it is we who can open or close the door. Kenya has become an African country.

My disagreements are not with the faith, but the Church has been very weak in its position on the colonial question; it has tended to defend the status quo.

Independence must be looked upon as a means to an end but not an end itself.

We have exploded once and for all the myth of white supremacy.

As to the future of white settlers, there's no room for anyone who does not believe in undiluted democracy. Those Europeans who hesitate have only one alternative, and that's to sell out and leave.

I am flattered by those who demand perfection from us. The paraphernalia of Western democracy are not necessarily best suited for Africa. New nations are bound to experiment with the institutions they inherit.

We must treat land as a national asset, encourage African ownership and cooperatives where necessary. We hope to acquire the land voluntarily—and pay fair value.

Either people trust us that we are sincere or there is very little that can be done.

Rule of this country by the majority is inevitable.

MARSHALL McLUHAN

𝕱 | *Marshall McLuhan, Canadian university professor,*
   | *writer, and lifelong student of communications and*
their effects, was born at Edmonton, Alberta, in 1911. His
father was a real estate and insurance broker and his mother
an actress. At the age of ten he made crystal sets for himself and his friends, and was thrilled when he was able to
pick up broadcasts from the United States.

He studied to become an engineer, but as he put it, "I
read my way out of engineering and into English literature."

McLuhan is an explorer of new frontiers in art, education,
philosophy, and sociology. He has proposed the theory that
many of the radical social changes that have taken place in
our time can be attributed to the effect of electronic com-
munications, especially radio, television, the movies, the
press, and advertising. "The medium is the message," he
asserts.

· · · · ·

Our "Age of Anxiety" is, in great part, the result of trying
to do today's job with yesterday's tools—with yesterday's
concepts.

The living room has become a voting booth. Participation

via television in Freedom Marches, in war, revolution, pollution, and other events is changing everything.

Too many people know too much about each other. . . . We have become irrevocably involved with, and responsible for, each other.

The "expert" is the man who stays put.

Medieval scholars were indifferent to the precise identity of the "books" they studied. In turn, they rarely signed even what was clearly their own. They were a humble service organization.

In television, images are projected at you. You are the screen. The images wrap around you.

The television generation is a grim bunch. It is much more serious than children of any other period—when they were frivolous, more whimsical. The television child is more earnest, more dedicated.

It is no longer convenient, or suitable, to use the latest technologies for fighting our wars, because the latest technologies have rendered war meaningless. The hydrogen bomb is history's exclamation point. It ends an age-long sentence of manifest violence!

MARGARET MEAD

☧ | *American anthropologist, born in 1901. She is associate*
   | *curator of the American Museum of Natural History*
in New York City. Widely traveled in remote areas of the
world, she has learned seven different primitive languages
and has written such widely acclaimed books on primitive
societies as *Coming of Age in Samoa, Growing Up in New
Guinea,* and *Sex and Temperament in Three Primitive
Societies.* Her book *Male and Female* concerns itself with
the plight of moderns. She has been principally interested
in studying how children and young people learn their cultures, and how these cultures change in adapting to the
modern world.

She has been honored for her achievements. In 1949 she
was elected "Outstanding Woman of the Year in Science"
by the Associated Press.

Her friends know her as a warm human being with an
open heart for all who inhabit the globe.

. . . . .

Europeans quickly learned to explore the universe with their
new instruments, and slowly they learned also that the new
knowledge of our solar system did not affect their faith.

Today it is well understood that a change in knowledge about the universe is not irreligious, that the keepers of man's faith can bless space exploration as once they blessed the ships that went to sea.

We can look around the world at other peoples to find out whether there are any people who have brought up their children without a knowledge of war. If we find such people —the Eskimo, for instance . . . then without making any new experiments we can say that human beings will *not* always, in all circumstances, go to war. Without knowing it, the Eskimo have made the experiment for us.

No science was possible until people could keep records, until observers could write down notes for themselves or for others to read and use later.

The anthropologist learns to eat all sorts of unfamiliar foods—dragonflies, octopus, blubber. He learns to sit in new positions which he may find very uncomfortable—cross-legged or squatting on one heel. All these things make it possible to understand the people better.

When a small group of primitive people give up their tribal religion and come into a world religion . . . the world religion may give them the feeling that all men, not just the people of their own village or tribe, are brothers.

Our first and most pressing problem is how to do away with warfare as a method of solving conflicts between national groups or between groups within a society who have different views about how the society is to be run.

As soon as a people have warfare and special weapons intended for use against other human beings . . . it becomes necessary to prevent members of the group from using such weapons against each other.

We have worked out international rules for publishing books, rules about ships from one part of the world that enter harbors in other parts of the world, rules for controlling the spread of disease from one country to another, and we have a world court and the idea for some kind of international police to keep peace in the world. And we can think ahead to a day when every human being will be a citizen of the earth who, if he is killed by another citizen, will have been murdered. All these ideas have now been invented.

Today, when a war might wipe out the whole human race, we need inventions to make warfare impossible.

The problem of getting rid of war comes first. But our success in doing this depends in part on our being able to solve several other problems at the same time. . . . In many parts of the world today millions of people live in poverty, hunger, sickness, and fear. For such people the idea of a quick and noble death, fighting for something—the ancient glory of their country, or the supposed superiority of one religious faith or of one "race" over another, or freedom from colonialism—might still seem preferable to the idea of working at the slower and harder task of finding peaceful solutions.

In the modern world we have invented ways of speeding up

invention, and people's lives change so fast that a person is born into one kind of world, grows up in another, and by the time his children are growing up, lives in still a different world.

In a world which is changing all the time no one's education is ever complete.

Once more we are entering a period in which men will have to give their whole attention to what they are doing and in which the safety of the whole group will depend on men and women who, as boys and girls, learned that life in the twentieth century is like a parachute jump: you have to get it right the first time.

GOLDA MEIR

Israeli leader and premier, born in Kiev, Russia, 1898. As a child she lived through tragic pogroms, during which she saw Cossacks murdering Jews and burning down their houses.

Then the family moved to the United States and Golda became a schoolteacher in Milwaukee, Wisconsin. In 1921 they moved to Palestine, where Mrs. Meir took part in the women's labor movement. She became a member of the Knesset, the parliament. She was the first Israeli Minister to Moscow, USSR, and later she became Israeli Minister of Labor. In 1956 she was made Minister for Foreign Affairs. During the Suez Canal crisis, she pleaded Israel's case before the United Nations General Assembly in New York. In 1969 she became Premier.

. . . . .

Those who wanted to destroy us thought that they would weaken us by persecution . . . but in so doing they could not help but strengthen the spirit of the people and steel us in our forward march.

We cannot afford to wage war without constructing.

Peace between nations and the observance of human rights are inseparable doctrines. Conversely, military aggression and minority oppression have proved themselves in the past to be linked in close and ominous kinship.

Man will conquer not other men but swamps and deserts and together create a world of free men and women toward which we all strive.

I desire only one thing more: to live only as long as I can live a full life in the State of Israel, and may I never lose the feeling that it is I who am indebted.

MARIANNE MOORE

A *poet of foremost standing in twentieth-century American literature, she was born in St. Louis, Missouri, in 1887.* As a young girl, she did not care much for poetry, but she loved books. At Bryn Mawr she spent most of her time in the biology laboratory, yet her first poems appeared in print in college publications. Soon she began to contribute to literary magazines and her poems appeared in book form.

Because of their wit, brevity, precision, and objectivity, Miss Moore's poems have been described as "encyclopedia articles set to music."

. . . . .

Why cannot money and life go for beauty instead of for war and intellectual oppression?

To earn a living is needful, but it can be done in routine ways.

Since writing is not only an art but a trade embodying principles attested by experience, we would do well not to forget that it is an expedient for making one's self understood and that what is said should at least have the air of having meant something to the person who wrote it.

Like dullness, implausibility obscures the point.

What do I mean by straight writing? . . . I mean, in part, writing that is not mannered, over-conscious, or at war with common sense.

Poetry watches life with affection.

I see no reason for calling my work poetry except that there is no other category in which to put it.

We are suffering from too much sarcasm.

It is a curiosity of literature how often what one says of another seems descriptive of one's self.

Don't look on art as effeminate, and museums as "the most tiring form of recreation."

I would, like Sir Winston Churchill, refuse to let betrayal rob me of trust in my fellow man.

Suppose you "don't believe in God," talk to someone very wise, who believed in God, did not, and then found that he did.

GAMAL ABDEL NASSER

✠ | *His name means "slave of the victorious." He was a*
| *Colonel in the Egyptian army; today he is President*
of the United Arab Republic.

Born in 1918, he was the son of a modest postmaster. At
sixteen, while a student in Cairo, he organized a schoolboy
riot.

He graduated from the Royal Military Academy as a
second lieutenant and, at the age of twenty-six, married the
daughter of a Cairo rug merchant.

In 1948 he was in the struggle against Israel and got
wounded in the shoulder; he stopped fighting only when
Cairo ordered him to do so.

Bitterly convinced that the real enemy was the corrupt
regime of Egypt, he organized the Free Officers, a secret
society, and led an army revolt that deposed King Farouk.
The United States offered him $1.3 billion to help build a
new Aswan dam. When Secretary Dulles withdrew the
offer, Nasser angrily nationalized the Suez Canal Company.
A war followed in 1956, and Nasser's armies were badly
beaten by the invading British, French, and Israelis.

The United Nations stopped the war and ordered the
withdrawal of the invading forces. To keep the peace, the

United Nations organized the first Emergency Force in history. This force patrolled the border between Egypt and Israel until 1967, when a new six-day war broke out. This war also ended with an Israeli victory. It was the third Arab-Israeli war. Anxiety continues to prevail over what may happen in that section of the world.

· · · · ·

The Americans want to give us aid and dominate our policy. I say we are sorry. We are ready to cut our rations and minimize the daily consumption so that we keep our independence.

Today we drink tea seven days a week. There is no need for that. We can drink it for five days only. We drink coffee for seven days; let us drink it for four. Meat, we can eat for three days only.

They say we have a supply crisis, but we do not tolerate any indignity. This is our character. We are people with dignity and we are not ready to sell it even for a billion pounds.

I have given the Egyptian people dignity.

(Someone asked him why he never delegates any authority. He replied:) Show me ten men I can trust.

Today, O my brothers, we are stronger than ever before. Arab unity has been unchained. The same flag of freedom that flies over Baghdad today will be hoisted in Amman and Beirut, just as it rose in every corner of the Arab world.

If we see today that America occupies Lebanon and Britain occupies Jordan, then I say: If they call for peace, we are for it. But if they are hostile toward us, we shall fight to the last drop of our blood. We shall not be terrorized by threats of fleets or atomic bombs. The leaders of the West must realize that Arab nationalism is very strong everywhere.

Arise, my brethren on the police force and in the army in Iraq! Stand side by side with your brothers and your people against your enemies. The freedom of Iraq is in your hands.

My brothers in Lebanon, there is no other way before you than the revolution to achieve your hopes. There is no other way but for you to rise and fight.

The spirits of Hitler and Mussolini have now entered the body of Secretary of State Dulles, who has now become a Nazi and a Fascist.

We cannot look at the map of the world without seeing our own place on it.

I maintain we are strong. The only trouble is, we do not realize just how strong we are.

Half the proved reserves of oil in the world lie beneath Arab soil. Have I made clear how great the importance of this element of strength is? So we are strong—strong not in the loudness of our voices when we wail or shout for help, but rather when we remain silent and . . . really understand the strength resulting from the ties binding us together.

The peoples of Africa will continue to look to us, who guard their northern gate and who constitute their link with all the outside world.

When I consider the eighty million Moslems in Indonesia and the fifty million in China, and the millions in Malaya, Siam and Burma, and the close to one hundred million in the Middle East, and the forty million inside the Soviet Union, and the other millions in far-flung parts of the world—when I consider these hundreds of millions united by a single creed, I emerge with a sense of the tremendous possibilities which we may realize through the cooperation of all these Moslems, a cooperation not going beyond the bounds of their natural loyalty to their own countries, yet enabling them and their brothers in faith to wield a power without limit.

I know everything that goes on in this country. I run everything myself.

REINHOLD NIEBUHR

✠ | *American clergyman, born in Wright City, Missouri,*
in 1892, son of the pastor of an Evangelical church.
He prepared for the ministry at Eden Theological Seminary
in St. Louis, then studied at Yale, where he took a B.D.
degree in 1914 and an M.A. degree in 1915.

For thirteen years he served as a pastor in the workers'
district of Detroit. In 1928 he was called to the Union
Theological Seminary in New York, where he lectured on
Christian ethics and philosophy of religion. He is the author
of several books dealing with religious and social questions,
such as *Moral Man and Immoral Society, Christianity and
Power Politics,* and *The Nature and Destiny of Man.*

. . . . .

Individualism understands only a part of man; collectivism
understands man only as a part. . . . Individualism sees man
only in relation to himself; but collectivism does not see
man at all, it sees only "society."

Nothing that is worth doing can be achieved in our lifetime; therefore we must be saved by hope. Nothing which
is true or beautiful or good makes complete sense in any

immediate context of history; therefore we must be saved by faith.

If we preach repentance, it must be repentance for those who accept the Lord as well as for those who pretend to deny Him.

If we preach the mercy of God, it must be with a humble recognition that we are in need of it as much as those who do not know God's mercy in Christ.

Intelligence will gradually soften prejudices and allay the conflict between Christianity and the Judaism out of which it emerged and with which it is organically related so that religions of the prophetic ideal may make common cause.

While no state can maintain its unity purely by coercion neither can it preserve itself without coercion.

The fact that the coercive factor in society is both necessary and dangerous seriously complicates the whole task of securing both peace and justice.

The common members of any national community, while sentimentally desiring peace, nevertheless indulge impulses of envy, jealousy, pride, bigotry, and greed, which make for conflict between communities.

There is always something abstract about justice. It tries to measure what cannot be measured. For neither the dimension of a great sin, nor the guiltiness of those who are implicated in it can be exactly measured, at least not by creatures who are unable to look into the secrets of the heart.

The selfishness of nations is proverbial. It was a dictum of George Washington that nations were not to be trusted beyond their own interest.

The necessity of using force in the establishment of unity in a national community, and the inevitable selfish exploitation of the instrument of coercion by the groups who wield them, adds to the selfishness of nations.

Perhaps the most significant moral characteristic of a nation is its hypocrisy.

There is no cure for the pride of a virtuous nation but pure religion.

For all the centuries of experience, men have not yet learned how to live together without compounding their vices and covering each other "with mud and with blood."

We know that we have the position which we hold in the world today partly by reason of factors and forces in the complex pattern of history which we did not create and from which we do not deserve to benefit. If we apprehend this religiously, the sense of destiny ceases to be a vehicle of pride and becomes the occasion for a new sense of responsibility.

JULIUS NYERERE

President of Tanzania, a country composed of the union of Tanganyika and Zanzibar.

Julius Nyerere was born in 1921 near Musoma, on the shores of Lake Victoria, into a pagan, tribal world. His father was chief of the Zanaki, a small Bantu tribe that filed the teeth of their young.

As a boy he was herding goats. At twelve he hiked from his village to the Roman Catholic secondary school to get a formal education. At Uganda's Makerere University he won first prize in a literary competition. After three years of teaching biology he obtained a scholarship to Edinburgh, and in 1949 he became the first Tanganyikan ever to study at a British university.

In 1954 he founded the party of Tanganyika African National Union, severed his tribal bonds and, in a battered car, began to tour the country, recruiting members for his organization and preaching a philosophy of nonviolence. In an election held in 1960, Nyerere's party won the victory, and he was asked to form a government. By 1961 Tanganyika was fully independent.

Contrary to the ways of other African leaders, who may call themselves "Redeemer" or "Lion of Malawi," Nyerere is known simply as Mwalimu—Swahili for teacher.

He is a rather frail man with a Chaplin-type moustache. He is married and the father of many children.

· · · · ·

Unless I can meet at least some of these aspirations, my head will roll just as surely as the tickbird follows the rhino.

I will never be a member of any government that discriminates against non-Africans.

It would be wrong of us to continue to distinguish between Tanganyikan citizens on any ground other than character and ability.

We cannot allow the growth of first- and second-class citizenship.

Often there is no room at first for a "loyal opposition," for its sole aim after independence could only be overthrow of the independence movement itself.

Violence is unnecessary and costly. Peace is the only way.

The African must and will rule. Our unity is our weapon.

We have changed our cry from *"Uhuru"* to *"Uhuru Na Kazi*—Freedom and Work.

JOSÉ CLEMENTE OROZCO

This Mexican painter was born in 1883. He was a contemporary of Siqueiros, Diego Rivera, Merida, and other muralists. He was trained as an architect; to turn into a muralist was a natural thing for him to do.

He believed that the mural is the most logical and the strongest form of art. It is also the most disinterested form —it is not for the enjoyment of the few, but is out in the open for the benefit of the many.

The New World, he felt, should develop its own new form of art, one that was not an imitation of Old World art or a copy of that of the Indians. The skycrapers of Manhattan, in his opinion, have nothing to do with the Egyptian pyramids or the Paris Opera; they are typically American.

Orozco spent some time living and working in the United States. His paintings can be seen at Dartmouth College, Pomona College, and the New School for Social Research in New York.

Yet no artist can break with his own heritage. Orozco remained a Mexican, just as Chagall remained a Russian, in his motives and feelings.

He died in 1949.

. . . . .

It seems that the line of Culture is continuous, without short cuts, unbroken from the unknown Beginning to the unknown End.

To go solicitously to Europe, bent on poking about its ruins in order to import them and servilely to copy them, is no greater error than is the looting of the indigenous remains of the New World with the object of copying with equal servility its ruins or its present folklore.

If new races have appeared upon the lands of the New World, such races have the unavoidable duty to produce a New Art in a new spiritual and physical medium. Any other road is plain cowardice.

VIJAYA LAKSHMI PANDIT

✿ *Indian nationalist leader, author, diplomat, and sister of Prime Minister Nehru, she was born in Allahabad,* India, in 1900. Her father, Motilal Nehru, was a well-to-do lawyer, and she was raised, amid opulence, by an English governess.

At her wedding, Mohandas K. Gandhi was among the guests. Her father and her brother had already become associated with this Indian leader in his struggle against British rule, and Mrs. Pandit joined the freedom movement. English prison soon became a second home to practically every member of the Nehru family. Mrs. Pandit was first imprisoned in 1932, when she was the mother of three daughters, the youngest only three.

In 1945 she was an observer at the San Francisco Conference, where the United Nations was born. India was not yet independent, but after independence, Mrs. Pandit became her country's ambassador. She was Ambassador to Washington and to London and to Moscow. She was the first woman to address the United Nations General Assembly.

. . . . .

Every seventh human being in the world is an Indian.

India . . . is not a mere geographical expression but a cultural concept and a distinctive way of life.

The spiritual and moral values which motivated the sages and philosophers of India through the long period of her recorded history have stood the test of time.

The emphasis on the unity of man and the unity of the universe has been ever present in the long march of the Indian people.

Hinduism cannot be described as a particular system of thought. Rather it is a commonwealth of systems; not a particular faith but a fellowship of faiths.

Democracy is not just a political creed. It is a way of life, and those who have accepted it are pledged to devote themselves "to promote social progress and better standards of life in larger freedom." (Quote from the United Nations Charter.)

Education . . . [is] not merely a means for earning a living or an instrument for the acquisition of wealth. "It is an initiation into the life of spirit, a training of the human soul in the pursuit of truth and the practice of virtue."

No nation has a monopoly of knowledge, it has become the common heritage of civilized man, but its fruits are available to us only through cooperation.

PABLO PICASSO

✢ *Spanish painter and sculptor, born in 1881, at Malaga, on the coast of Spain.* His father was an art teacher at the Barcelona Academy of Fine Arts.

In 1900 he went to Paris, and has remained in France ever since.

At first he worked in many styles, painting clowns, harlequins, and beggars in realistic manner. Later he became interested in African sculptures, and this led him to "cubism." He was the founder of that school of art, which reduces images to geometric shapes, planes, and angles.

However, Picasso has never restricted himself to any style but has retained his versatility, painting as a classicist, a realist, a cubist, and a surrealist—and always as an experimenter.

. . . . .

In my opinion to search means nothing in painting. To think is the thing. Nobody is interested in following a man who, with his eyes fixed on the ground, spends his life looking for the pocketbook that fortune should put in his path.

They speak of naturalism in opposition to modern painting. I would like to know if anyone has ever seen a natural work of art. Nature and art, being two different things, cannot be the same thing.

To me there is no past or future in art. If a work of art cannot live always in the present it must not be considered at all. The art of the Greeks, of the Egyptians, of the great painters who lived in other times, is not an art of the past; perhaps it is more alive today than it ever was.

Whenever I had something to say I have said it in the manner in which I have felt it ought to be said. Different motives inevitably require different methods of expression.

What a miserable fate for a painter who adores blondes to have to stop himself putting them into a picture because they don't go with the basket of fruit!

I put all the things I like into my pictures. The things— so much the worse for them; they just have to put up with it.

A painter paints to unload himself of feelings and visions.

Everyone wants to understand art. Why not try to understand the song of a bird? Why does one love the night, flowers, everything around one, without trying to understand them?

People who try to explain pictures are usually barking up the wrong tree.

HYMAN RICKOVER

The son of a poor Jewish tailor in Chicago, Rickover was to build the world's first atomic submarine. He was born in Russian Poland in 1900, and came to the United States with his family in 1904. As soon as he was old enough, Hyman began to work as a messenger for Western Union. He delivered telegrams after school, then worked at his homework until long past midnight. He went to the United States Naval Academy in Annapolis because the education there was free.

He was not a popular boy: he was bookish, hard-working, and critical, taking little part in athletics or in social doings. He specialized in electrical engineering and, at the Navy's expense, went to Columbia, where he earned a master's degree. At Columbia he met his future wife.

The only seagoing command he ever held was on a rickety minesweeper on the China station. But early in World War II, while still a Lieutenant-Commander, he became Chief of the Electrical Section of the Navy's Bureau of Ships. There he was known for his efficiency and also for his talent for making enemies.

In 1946 he was sent to Oak Ridge to study atomic energy. There he soon concluded that the future of the Navy lay in nuclear propulsion, and that the most suitable vessel to begin the conversion to nuclear energy was the submarine. His vision was not shared by his superiors, and in the end he was recalled and assigned to some vague duties.

But while Rickover was making powerful enemies in the Navy, he was also making powerful friends in the Senate, who understood and supported his aspirations. His efforts led to the launching of the first atomic submarine, the *Nautilus*. In its work with such vessels, the United States is far ahead of the Soviet Union.

Rickover is summoned frequently to the Capitol to testify, but rarely does he present the customary prepared statement, preferring to await questions, which he answers with his customary bluntness.

"Haven't you prepared for this hearing?" a Congressman once asked him.

"Certainly," said Rickover, "I shaved and put on a clean shirt."

· · · · ·

The more you sweat in peace the less you bleed in war.

A military organization is set up to do routine, not imaginative work. . . . If anyone comes along with a new idea, the people in the organization naturally tend to make him conform. The first thing a man has to do is make up his mind that he is going to get his head chopped off ultimately. If he has that feeling, perhaps he can accomplish something.

Superefficient "administrators" are the curse of the country. Their main function seems to be to harass brainworkers with trivia and to waste as much time as possible.

Much of our technology is only empiricism. We know an automobile engine works, but we don't know why. We go along by trial and error, turning out enormous quantities of goods without understanding the basic principles involved.

(About young engineers he said:) They know a lot of facts, but few principles. They simply are not educated.

Today everybody is an expert on nuclear reactors. Everybody has an idea that will work better, on paper, than ours. These guys will go to someone in authority, the Chief of Naval Operations or even the Secretary of the Navy, and say, "Why doesn't Rickover try this?" We have to examine and answer every one of these helpful suggestions and so spend half our time fielding foul balls. If they would only leave us alone, we could get the job done a hell of a lot faster and better.

It has been drummed into us that we have some God-given superiority in our way of doing things. This is not true, and some changes are in order. We must stop depending on routine production systems and methods. The nuclear age demands much better technology than we are now using. And we must cut out the organizational red tape and get down to fundamentals. The man running a factory or a project must keep himself personally informed of what is actually going on. He can't rely on progress reports from underlings.

If the Russians would send a man to hell, we'd say "We can't let them beat us to it!"

The most pressing problem is . . . education.

You people set up laws on what is to go in people's mouths, but you won't even set up recommendations on what goes into their minds.

Most Americans seem to regard education as a commodity or service which anybody ought to get, simply by paying tuition or by having the cost of education met through taxes.

A school system that insists on the same instruction for the talented, average, and below-average child may prevent as many children from growing intellectually as would a system that excludes children because of social, political, or economic status of parents. Neither system is democratic.

ANNA ELEANOR ROOSEVELT

✠ *Wife of Franklin D. Roosevelt, thirty-second President of the United States.*

Anna Eleanor Roosevelt was born in 1884. Her mother died when she was eight, and her father just two years later. She was raised by her grandmother. In a family of pretty Roosevelt girls she was called "the ugly duckling" and was told that probably no one would ever want to marry her. Yet she got the handsomest Roosevelt boy, her fifth cousin, Franklin Delano. They were married in 1905, while Franklin was still a student at the Columbia Law School, and Eleanor's uncle, President Theodore Roosevelt, gave the bride away. It was Uncle Teddy, not the bridal couple, who was the center of attraction at the reception, as he stood among a crowd of guests, who were laughing loudly at his stories.

As a young girl, Eleanor did social work. When Franklin became President, she continued to be interested in social problems as First Lady. She lectured widely, wrote a daily newspaper column and a number of books. During World War II, she visited the troops in England, the southwest Pacific, and the Caribbean.

After her husband's death, President Truman asked her

to serve as a member of the United States delegation to the first United Nations General Assembly in London. Later she was appointed Chairman of the Commission on Human Rights, drawing up the Universal Declaration of Human Rights, which was adopted by the General Assembly, December 10, 1948. With the election of President Eisenhower in 1952, she resigned as delegate to the United Nations.

During the next five years she circled the globe three times. She visited Nehru in India, talked to the Emperor and Empress of Japan, and swam in the Adriatic with President Tito of Yugoslavia. While in the Soviet Union, she chatted for two and a half hours with Nikita Khrushchev.

She was a remarkable lady who, with a happy balance of idealism and practical common sense, helped to shape history. She died in 1962.

· · · · ·

Only man is able to record his experiences and leave a written record of his accomplishments and his failures.

The loftiest sentiments and most noble purposes of man have usually been expressed by the great men of history in the simplest and most direct way.

True hospitality comes from the heart, and is not the product of ostentatious and expensive material surroundings.

No one can make you feel inferior without your consent.

You gain strength, courage, and confidence by every experience in which you really stop to look fear in the face. You are able to say to yourself, "I have lived through this horror. I can take the next thing that comes along." . . . You must do the thing you think you cannot do.

Life was meant to be lived, and curiosity must be kept alive. One must never, for whatever reason, turn his back on life.

Without the ability to be gay and to treat serious things lightly after the serious thinking is done and the decisions reached, I doubt whether any man could long carry the job of being President of the United States.

One's philosophy is not best expressed in words; it is expressed in the choices one makes. . . . In the long run, we shape our lives and we shape ourselves. The process never ends until we die. And the choices we make are ultimately our responsibility.

FRANKLIN DELANO ROOSEVELT

☨ | *Thirty-second President of the United States, the only*
☨ | *president to be elected for four terms: in 1932, 1936,*
1940, and 1944. He was born in 1882 at Hyde Park, New
York, the only child of Sara Delano and James Roosevelt,
a wealthy railroad and shipping man.

At Groton School he was considered an "intelligent and
faithful scholar, and a good boy" though "athletically . . .
rather too slight for success." At Harvard his grades were
about average. At twenty-one, he had fallen in love with
his fifth cousin, Anna Eleanor Roosevelt. In 1905 they
were married.

In 1907 FDR finished his law studies and joined a law
firm. But he wanted to be more than, as he described himself, a "full-fledged office boy." Thus, when the Democratic
Party of Dutchess County, New York, offered him the
nomination as state senator, he accepted it, and his political career began. He served two terms as senator in Al-
bany. In 1912 he supported the candidacy of Woodrow
Wilson. When Wilson was elected President, he offered
Roosevelt the job of Undersecretary of the Navy. In 1920
he ran for the office of Vice-President, supporting Wilson's
League of Nations, and suffered a thrashing defeat. He
spent the following year as a "full-fledged office boy."

Then, in the summer of 1921, after a quick swim in icy water, he was stricken with polio. Never again could he stand unaided on his feet.

His mother wanted him to retire and spend the rest of his life as an invalid, but by 1928 he was back in politics. He was elected Governor of New York. When a Republican newspaper attacked the former Governor, Al Smith, for having drafted a "sick man," Smith retorted, "A Governor does not have to be an acrobat." Roosevelt served two terms as Governor.

On March 4, 1933, his hand on the ancient Dutch Bible that had been in the Roosevelt family for three centuries, he took the oath as the thirty-second President of the United States. The country was struggling to recover from a severe economic depression, and in his acceptance speech Roosevelt pledged himself "to a New Deal for the American people" and promised aid to the "forgotten man." He surrounded himself with young intellectuals, dubbed by the press "the Brain Trust," to deal with the grave problems of bringing prosperity back again.

In 1939, as he saw the storm clouds of war gathering, he asked Hitler and Mussolini for pledges against aggression. Hitler answered with a sneer, Mussolini by poking fun at the President's illness. On December 6 he addressed a personal peace message to Emperor Hirohito of Japan. But on December 7, 1941, Japan attacked Pearl Harbor, and Congress declared war on Japan.

During World War II he worked for the unity of the Big Three: Great Britain, the Soviet Union, and the United States. He traveled across the world to meet with Churchill and Stalin—to Casablanca, Cairo, Teheran, Yalta. He spoke eloquently of human freedom, and labored to create the

United Nations. He died suddenly in 1945, a few weeks before the drafting of the United Nations Charter began, and not quite a month before Nazi Germany surrendered.

He was buried in the garden at Hyde Park where he once played as a child. "A plain white monument—no carving or decoration" was placed over his grave, as he had wanted it. The nation and the world lamented his passing.

· · · · ·

The only thing we have to fear is fear itself.

To some generations much is given. Of other generations of Americans much is expected. This generation of Americans has a rendezvous with history.

Here in America we are waging a great and successful war. . . . It is a war for the survival of democracy.

Government is not like a doughnut. . . . It cannot have an empty space in the middle, but must be an entirety.

The Democratic Party and the Republican Party should not be merely Tweedledum and Tweedledee to each other.

The common denominator of our great men in public life has not been mere allegiance to one political party, but the disinterested devotion with which they have tried to serve the whole country.

Our democratic army has existed for one purpose only: the defense of our freedom.

The life of a nation is the fullness of the measure of its will to live.

We must be the great arsenal of democracy.

Yesterday, December 7, 1941—a date which will live in infamy—the United States was suddenly and deliberately attacked by naval and air forces of the Empire of Japan. . . . There is no blinking of the fact that our people, our territory, and our interest are in grave danger.

With confidence in our armed forces—with the unbounding determination of our people—we will gain the inevitable triumph, so help us God.

The militarists of Berlin and Tokyo started this war. But the massed, angered forces of common humanity will finish it.

These Republican leaders have not been content with attacks upon me, or my wife, or my sons—they now include my little dog Fala. Unlike the members of my family, he resents this. Being a Scottie, as soon as he learned that the Republican fiction writers had concocted a story that I had left him behind on an Aleutian Island and had sent a destroyer back to find him at a cost to the taxpayers of two or three million dollars, his Scotch soul was furious. He has not been the same dog since.

When it comes to baseball, I am the kind of fan who wants to get plenty of action for his money. . . . I must confess that I get the biggest kick out of the biggest score.

I honestly feel it would be best for the country to keep baseball going.

When you get to the end of your rope, tie a knot and hang on.

A conservative is a man with two perfectly good legs who has never learned to walk.

A radical is a man with both feet firmly planted in the air.

A reactionary is a somnambulist walking backwards.

The test of our progress is not whether we add more to the abundance of those who have much; it is whether we provide enough for those who have too little.

We shall have to take the responsibility for world collaboration, or we shall have to bear the responsibility for another world conflict.

BERTRAND, LORD RUSSELL

☥ | *English philosopher, mathematician, author, and so-
cial reformer, born in 1872. Lord Russell is a remark-*
able teacher, who has lectured at practically every university
from Cambridge to Peking, from Harvard to Upsala. Med-
als and honors, including the Nobel Prize, have been
showered on him. Like other great men of our day he was
also suspended and jailed a couple of times.

He wrote his own obituary in a mocking, self-deprecat-
ing vein, and added to it the footnote, "This obituary will
(or will not) be published in *The Times* for June 1, 1962,
on the occasion of my lamented but belated death." However, he was wrong in predicting the date of his death, for
in 1969 he was still very much alive and active, though
nearing one hundred years.

Here are some excerpts from his ironical self-appraisal,
written in the third person:

"His grandfather, Lord John Russell, the Victorian Prime
Minister, visited Napoleon in Elba; his maternal grandmother was a friend of the Young Pretender's widow." At
"the age of 18 . . .he entered Trinity College, Cambridge,
becoming . . . a Fellow in 1895. During the fifteen years
that followed, he produced the books upon which his repu-

tation in the learned world was based: *The Foundation of Geometry, The Philosophy of Leibnitz, The Principles of Mathematics.* . . . His . . . lack of spiritual depth became painfully evident during the First World War, when Russell . . . perversely maintained that, war being an evil, the aim of statesmanship should have been to bring the war to an end as soon as possible. . . . It must be supposed that mathematical studies had caused him to take a wrongly quantitative view which ignored the question of principle involved. . . . Trinity College, very properly, deprived him of his lectureship, and for some months of 1918 he was in prison. . . .

"In 1920 he paid a brief visit to Russia, whose government did not impress him favorably. . . . In subsequent years his energies were dissipated in writings advocating socialism, educational reform, and a less rigid code of morals as regards to marriage. . . .

"In the Second World War he took no public part, having escaped to a neutral country just before its outbreak. In private conversation he was wont to say that homicidal lunatics were employed in killing each other, but that sensible men would keep out of their way while they were doing it. Fortunately this outlook . . . has become rare in this age, which recognizes that heroism has value independent of its utility. . . . His principles were curious, but, such as they were, governed his actions."

And they still do. At ninety-five, Bertrand Russell was agitating against the war in Vietnam, demonstrating and disrupting traffic at Trafalgar Square, from whence policemen carried him tenderly to jail—in sitting position, lest they break his brittle bones.

. . . . .

Three passions, simple but overwhelmingly strong, have governed my life: the longing for love, the search for knowledge, and unbearable pity for the suffering of mankind.

I have sought love . . . because in the union of love I have seen, in a mystic miniature, the prefiguring vision of the heaven the saints and poets have imagined.

With equal passion I have sought knowledge. I have wished to understand the hearts of men. I have wished to know why the stars shine.

Love and knowledge, so far as they were possible, led upward toward the heavens, but always pity brought me back to earth. Echoes of cries, of pain, reverberate in my heart. Children in famine, victims tortured by oppressors, helpless old people a hated burden to their sons, and the whole world of loneliness, poverty, and pain make a mockery of what human life should be. I long to alleviate the evil, but I cannot, and I too suffer.

For six years the civilized nations of the world devoted their best energies to killing each other, and they find it difficult suddenly to switch over to keeping each other alive.

Even when the experts all agree, they may well be mistaken.

The most important evils that mankind have to consider are those which they inflict upon each other through stupidity or malevolence or both.

When a man tortures himself he feels that it gives him a right to torture others.

Pride of race is even more harmful than national pride.

The Greeks held that slavery was justifiable so long as the masters were Greek and the slaves barbarians, but that otherwise it was contrary to nature.

I remember once going to a place where they kept a number of pedigreed bulls, and what made a bull illustrious was the milk-giving qualities of his female ancestors. But if bulls had drawn up the pedigrees they would have been very different. Nothing would have been said about the female ancestors, except that they were docile and virtuous, whereas the male ancestors would have been celebrated for their supremacy in battle.

Men of science at their best have a special kind of impressiveness, resulting from the combination of great intellect with childlike simplicity. When I say "simplicity" I do not mean anything involving lack of cleverness; I mean the habit of thinking impersonally, without regard for the worldly advantage or disadvantage of an opinion or an action. Among the men of science I have known, Einstein is the supreme example of this quality.

It is preoccupation with possessions, more than anything else, that prevents men from living freely and nobly.

Hatred of enemies is easier and more intense than love of friends. But from men who are more anxious to injure opponents than to benefit the world at large no great good is to be expected.

It is clear that many men willingly forgo wealth for the sake of power and glory, and that nations habitually sacrifice riches to rivalry with other nations.

Marxians never sufficiently recognize that love of power is quite as strong a motive, and quite as great a source of injustice, as love of money.

In England men have reached the point of suspecting a good speaker, but if a man speaks badly they think he must be honest.

The civilized nations have accepted democratic government as a method of settling internal disputes without violence.

Civilization is not so stable that it cannot be broken up; and a condition of lawless violence is not one out of which any good thing is likely to emerge. For this reason, if for no other, revolutionary violence in a democracy is infinitely dangerous.

Intelligence languishes where thought is not free.

Some people believe that by living on sour milk one can achieve immortality.

I do not think that mere inequality of wealth, in itself, is a very grave evil. If everybody had enough, the fact that some have more than enough would be unimportant.

Good relations between individuals, freedom from hatred and violence and oppression, general diffusion of education, leisure rationally employed, the progress of art and science—these are among the most important ends that a political theory ought to have in view.

CARL SANDBURG

✝ | *This American author, poet, lecturer, singer of folk*
  | *songs, and collector of ballads was born in Galesburg,*
Illinois, in 1878. Throughout his youth he worked very hard
at any job he could get, with little time for education. After
fighting in the Spanish-American War, he was persuaded
by someone in the ranks to go to college. *Chicago Poems*
(1916) was his first poetry collection. There have been
many more since then.

It may have been having Illinois as a birthplace that inspired him to write his monumental biography of Abraham
Lincoln. He also wrote children's books, including *Rootabaga Stories*, *Rootabaga Pigeons*, and *The Rootabaga
Country*.

With his guitar, his intractable white lock falling onto
his brow, he often appeared on television, singing ballads
in a rich, deep voice with a modest range. He was a simple,
rustic, good man. He died in 1967.

．　．　．　．　．

I tell you the past is a bucket of ashes.

Slang is a language that takes off its coat, spits on its hands,
and goes to work.

The republic is a dream. Nothing happens unless first a dream.

I won't take my religion from any man who never works except with his mouth.

Look out how you use proud words. When you let proud words go, it is not easy to call them back.

When Abraham Lincoln was shoveled into the tombs, he forgot the copperheads and the assassin . . . in the dust, in the cool tombs.

JEAN PAUL SARTRE

✠ | *French writer and philosopher, whose ideas have be-
come known as existentialism.*

He was born in Paris in 1905, and was a brilliant student.
He became a teacher of philosophy, first at a lycée, or high
school, at Le Havre, later in the Lycée Condorcet in Paris.
Sartre wrote his first novel in 1938. During World War II,
while playing an active role in the French resistance to
German occupation, he wrote his first plays, *The Flies* and
No Exit. In 1945 he visited the United States and was
favorably impressed, liking New York in particular.

Today Sartre devotes himself entirely to writing. He is
very prolific. In addition to plays, novels, stories, and essays,
he is director of an existentialist review, *Les Temps Mo-
dernes.*

. . . . .

To be sure, the book is the noblest, the most ancient of
forms; to be sure, we will always have to return to it.

The film, by its very nature, speaks to crowds: it speaks to
them about crowds and about their destiny.

The radio surprises people at the table or in bed, at the moment when they are most defenseless.

It is improper for us to stoop in order to please.

We always choose the good, and nothing can be good for us without being good for all.

The freedom of writing implies the freedom of the citizen. One does not write for slaves. The art of prose is bound up with the only regime in which prose has meaning, democracy.

The essence of the lie implies that the liar actually is in complete possession of the truth which he is hiding.

Man is nothing else but what he makes of himself. . . . He is therefore nothing else than the ensemble of his acts, nothing else than his life.

Each man must discover his own way.

Nations today are separated by difference of economic and military potential more surely than by seas or mountains.

It is not rare that one chooses a life of passion rather than one of reason.

A right is nothing more than the other aspect of duty.

ALBERT SCHWEITZER

☧ | *Alsatian philosopher, theologian, author, and organ*
| *virtuoso—in each of these fields, had he so desired, he*
could have risen to fame and fortune, but deeply touched by
human suffering, he started, late in life, a new career as a
medical missionary in Equatorial Africa.

Schweitzer was born in 1875, in Upper Alsace. His father
was a clergyman. His paternal grandfather had been a
schoolmaster and organist, and three of his brothers occupied similar posts. His mother was the daughter of a pastor.
In 1916, during World War I, his mother, walking on the
road, was knocked down and killed by galloping cavalry
horses. Such a tragedy would be enough to turn any man
into a pacifist.

At school Schweitzer was at first a poor scholar, but he
became interested in history and the natural sciences, and
then, at Strasbourg University, took up theology and
philosophy. Nor did he neglect his organ lessons.

In 1899 he obtained a post at the Church of St. Nicholas
in Strasbourg, serving first as a deacon, later as a curate.
While there, he began to write books of monumental
length about music and about Christianity. At the same

time he was lecturing at Strasbourg University and giving organ concerts. With all these occupations, he still found time to write a pamphlet about organ building.

Then, in 1905, at the height of his success, one Friday the thirteenth, the day that is supposed to bring bad luck, it struck him as incomprehensible that he should be allowed to lead such a happy life while so many people struggled and suffered. Following this revelation he took charge of abandoned or neglected children. Then he became concerned with tramps and discharged prisoners. Finally, he resolved to go to Africa and become a jungle doctor.

However, Schweitzer had no medical degree, and so, at the age of thirty, he became a medical student at the University of Strasbourg, where he was also a professor.

After seven years he got his doctor's degree and was ready to go to Africa, although his friends suggested that he should first have his head examined by his colleagues. Nevertheless, he offered his services to the Paris Missionary Society and in February, 1913, with seventy packing cases, he embarked for Lambaréné, in the French colony of Gabon.

On his arrival he set up a consulting office in an old henhouse. Since he was the first doctor in the region to use anesthetics, he soon gained a reputation among the natives as a wonder doctor, who first put his patients to death, then resuscitated them and made them healthy.

In 1914 World War I broke out. As Alsace was at that time German territory, Dr. Schweitzer was arrested as an "enemy alien," deported to France, and later sent back to Alsace.

After the war Schweitzer returned to Lambaréné and never again left it except to go on lecture tours or to give organ recitals to collect money for his hospital.

Albert Schweitzer's philosophy could be summed up in his own words: *Reverence for Life*. By this he meant all life—man, beasts, birds, and insects. Dining in Lambaréné, he threw crumbs on the floor for the ants. He was a man of great physical force, as well as being a great mystic—one of the few who do not merely talk about religion but put it into service.

He died, in 1965, at the age of ninety.

. . . . .

If anyone assures me that he has two languages, each as thoroughly familiar to him as the other, I immediately ask him in which of them he counts and reckons, in which he can best give me the names of kitchen utensils and tools used by carpenter or smith, and in which of them he dreams. I have not yet come across anyone who, when thus tested, had not to admit that one of the languages occupied only a second place.

Truth is under all circumstances more valuable than non-truth, and this must apply to the truth in the realm of history as to other kinds of truth.

In reliance upon the elementary truth which is embodied in the idea of the "Brotherhood of those who bear the mark of pain," I ventured to found the Forest Hospital at Lambaréné. That truth was recognized, and is now spreading.

I wanted to be a doctor that I might be able to work without having to talk.

Anyone who proposes to do good must not expect people to roll stones out of his way, but must accept his lot calmly if they even roll a few more upon it.

Everyone shall exert himself in that state of life in which he is placed, to practice true humanity toward his fellow men, on that depends the future of mankind.

No fate can prevent a man from giving others his human service side by side with his life work.

The tragic fact is that the interests of colonization and those of civilization do not always run parallel.

It is unthinkable that we civilized peoples should keep for ourselves alone the wealth of means for fighting sickness, pain, and death which science has given us.

The real savages . . . had a quite different conception of a present. When on the point of leaving the hospital cured, they used to demand one from me, because I had now become their friend.

The spirit of the age . . . is filled with disdain for thinking.

Renunciation of thinking is a declaration of spiritual bankruptcy.

Denouncing all hope of self-discovered truth, men will end by accepting as truth what is forced upon them with authority and by propaganda.

Sincerity is the foundation of the spiritual life.

To the man who is truly ethical all life is sacred, including that which from the human point of view seems lower in the scale.

I rejoice over the new remedies for sleeping sickness, which enable me to preserve life, whereas I had previously to watch a painful disease. But every time I have under the microscope the germs which cause the disease, I cannot but reflect that I have to sacrifice this life in order to save other life.

Devoted as I was from boyhood to the cause of the protection of animal life, it is a special joy to me that the universal ethic of Reverence for Life shows the sympathy with animals, which is so often represented as sentimentality, to be a duty which no thinking man can escape.

When will the time come when public opinion will tolerate no longer any popular amusements which depend on the ill treatment of animals?

Christianity cannot take the place of thinking, but it must be founded on it.

Only through love that we can attain to communion with God.

It seemed to me a matter of course that we should all take our share of the burden of pain which lies upon the world.

Because I have confidence in the power of truth and of spirit, I believe in the future of mankind.

White and colored must meet in an atmosphere of the ethical spirit. Then only will natural understanding be possible.

GEORGE BERNARD SHAW

British playwright, novelist, critic, satirist, social re-former. He was born in Dublin, Ireland, in 1856. His father was an alcoholic; his mother left home and, with her three daughters, went to live in London, leaving George behind. For six years she did not write to him. Shaw attributed his mocking nature to his unfortunate childhood. He said, "If you cannot get rid of the family skeleton, make it dance."

Shaw left school at fourteen for the job of office boy in a land agent's office. At twenty he moved to London to become a writer. Some of his first novels were published in obscure Socialist journals. At twenty-nine he began to write musical and dramatic criticism, and at forty-two, in collaboration with William Archer, he became a playwright. His plays were read with delight, but none were performed until some of them were produced in the United States and in Germany.

Shaw was a master of witty dialogue and stagecraft. He provided his plays with brilliantly written introductions, some almost as long as the plays themselves. Among his famous plays are *Saint Joan, Man and Superman,* and

Pygmalion, on which the popular musical *My Fair Lady* is based.

He was a tall, lean, muscular man, with a ruddy complexion and red hair and whiskers, which eventually turned white. He was a vegetarian, a teetotaler, and a militant Socialist, and he was as shy as he was waspish and severe. He died in 1950.

. . . . .

The liar's punishment is not in the least that he is not believed, but that he cannot believe anyone else.

Honest government is impossible without honest schools; for honest schools are illegal under dishonest governments.

To teach either Latin versification or the Marxist dialectic to children who should be learning arts and crafts is as wasteful and mischievous as teaching trades or crafts to pupils who are keen on mathematics, history, or language, but have hardly enough manual dexterity to sharpen their pencils or lace their shoes securely.

Napoleon was a contemporary of Kant, Goethe, Mozart, and Beethoven. Compare their tombs, and you will get an aesthetic measure of how much more we admire a great soldier than a great philosopher, poet, or composer.

Adolf Hitler . . . was lord of half Europe whilst Einstein was an exile, with much smaller income than a baseball champion.

Every war is a war to end war and to save civilization; we go on killing one another and glorifying our successful commanders as before.

Elementary civilization is impossible without a moral code like the Ten Commandments.

Our schools must inculcate political principles, manners, morals, and religion.

England and America are two countries separated by the same language.

I enjoy convalescence; it is the part that makes the illness worthwhile.

The most anxious man in a prison is the warden.

Patriotism is your conviction that this country is superior to all other countries because you were born in it.

Youth is a wonderful thing; what a crime to waste it on children.

I am not a friend of the poor and an enemy of the rich as ignorant people expect a Socialist to be.

It was proposed that Queen Elizabeth should marry Ivan the Terrible. . . . Either they would have separated pretty promptly or else Ivan would now be known as Ivan the Terrified.

You cannot make a silk purse out of a sow's ear except in a plastic factory.

When a man wants to murder a tiger he calls it sport; when a tiger wants to murder him, he calls it ferocity.

Nietzsche defined nations as people who read the same newspapers.

Art, science, and religion are really identical and inseparable in their foundations.

The fear of government may be the beginning of civilization just as the fear of God is the beginning of wisdom.

There is only one religion, though there are a hundred versions of it.

GERTRUDE STEIN

This American poet and lecturer was born in 1874. She was educated at Radcliffe College, and for a while attended Johns Hopkins Medical School, where she specialized in brain anatomy.

In 1904, she moved to Paris. A stocky little woman with a round face and a boyish haircut, she became a familiar figure, walking her white poodles on the Montparnasse. There she became interested in painting and met the modern artists, Matisse and Picasso, whose biographies she wrote.

She developed her own style of poetry, using words often for their sound, rather than for their sense. Her most quoted line is, "A rose is a rose is a rose is a rose." In addition to poems, biographies, and other prose, she wrote a libretto for an opera, *Four Saints in Three Acts*. She lectured at Cambridge, at Oxford, and at many American universities. During World War II she nursed the French wounded and, at the end of the war, was decorated by the French government.

She died in 1946.

. . . . .

The pleasure of a literature is having it all inside you. It is the one thing that one can have inside you.

English grammar is interesting because it is so simple. Once you really know how to diagram a sentence really know it, you know practically all you have to know about English grammar . . . so why make a fuss about it?

A private life is the long thick tree and the private life is the life for me.

A frog hopping he cannot ever hop exactly the same distance or the same way of hopping at every hop. A bird's singing is perhaps the nearest thing to repetition but if you listen they too vary their insistence.

A motor goes inside and the car goes on, but my business my ultimate business as an artist was not with where the car goes as it goes but with the movement inside that is of the essence of its going.

What does a comma do? I have refused them so often and left them out so much and did without them so continually that I have come finally to be indifferent to them.

A comma by helping you along holding your coat for you and putting on your shoes keeps you from living your life as actively as you should lead it.

If you read older books you will see that they do pretty well what they please with capital and small letters and I have always felt that one does do pretty well what one pleases with capitals and small letters.

Battles are named because there have been hills which have made a hill in a battle.

Poetry is I say essentially a vocabulary just as prose is essentially not.

Poetry is concerned with using with abusing, with losing with wanting, with denying with avoiding with adoring with replacing the noun.

ADLAI E. STEVENSON

☩ | *American lawyer, politician, Governor of the state of*
Illinois, twice Democratic candidate for the presi-
dency, he was United States Ambassador to the United
Nations when he died. A man of thought in an age of
action, he was an eloquent spokesman for liberalism, with
a rare sense of humor and true humility.

Mr. Stevenson was born in 1900, in Los Angeles, where
his father was, at the time, an executive for the Hearst
newspapers. He was the grandson of a Vice-President of the
United States, Adlai Stevenson, who held the office during
Grover Cleveland's second term. On his mother's side he
was the grandson of Jesse Fell, who was the first person to
propose Abraham Lincoln for the presidency.

Mr. Stevenson began his political career in 1933 when,
as a bright young lawyer, he moved to Washington to work
for President Franklin D. Roosevelt. In 1945 he was representative to the San Francisco Conference, where the
United Nations was born, and senior adviser to the American delegation at the first meeting of the General Assembly,
held in London in 1946.

In 1960 President-elect Kennedy offered him the post of

chief delegate of the United States Mission to the United Nations. He was still holding that office when he died in 1965 on a London street.

He was a tense man with a solid handshake and a ready smile, a man of wisdom and warmth, who was fully dedicated to the cause of peace and justice for all men.

· · · · ·

Friendship is the greatest enrichment that I have found.

When I was a boy I never had much sympathy for a holiday speaker. He was just a kind of interruption between the hot dogs, a fly in the lemonade.

Communism is the corruption of a dream of justice.

I don't believe irresponsible promises are good politics. Promise-peddling and double talk may be expedient and catch some votes from the unwary and innocent, but promises also have a way of coming home to roost.

The First World War was a shock, but not a lesson.

Eggheads unite! You have nothing to lose but your yolks.

If Communism is a problem for the United Nations, so is the United Nations a problem for Communism. The United Nations is a community of tolerance, and a community of tolerance is a terrible frustration to the totalitarian mind.

The art of government has grown from its seeds in the tiny
city-states of Greece to become the political mode of half
the world. So let us dream of a world in which all states,
great and small, work together for the peaceful flowering of
the republic of man.

EDWARD TELLER

Hungarian-American physicist, referred to as "the father of the hydrogen bomb."

Born in 1908, he finally left Hungary, because Jews were often not permitted to study there. He continued his education at the Institute of Technology at Karlsruhe and at Leipzig, both in Germany, and at Yale. Since 1935, he has taught physics at several American universities.

Teller was involved in the early planning of the atomic bomb, and worked at the Los Alamos Laboratory, under the direction of Robert Oppenheimer. He was his principal protagonist in the controversy over the building of the hydrogen bomb.

He was not present when, on November 1, 1952, the first hydrogen bomb, "Mike," was exploded in the Pacific. He was watching it at Berkeley on the seismograph—a sensitive recording instrument that writes the earth's tremors on a photographic film with the help of a fine beam of light.

Teller received the Fermi award of $50,000 in 1962.

· · · · ·

A modern technical and scientific development is rightly considered a wonderfully complex and difficult undertaking.

. . . Hundreds of ideas and thousands of technicals skills are required for success. The hydrogen bomb is an achievement of this kind. It is the work of many excellent people who were all essential for the final outcome.

The story that is often presented to the public is quite different. One hears of a brilliant idea and only too often the name of a single individual is mentioned. This picture is both untrue and unjust.

To develop the [atomic] bomb was right. To drop it was wrong. We could have used the bomb to end the war without bloodshed by exploding it high over Tokyo at night without prior warning. . . . We could then have said to the Japanese leaders: "This was an atomic bomb. One of them can destroy a city. Surrender or be destroyed!"

I believe they would have surrendered just as they did following the destruction of the two cities. If that had happened it would have been a tremendous moral as well as military victory. We could have said to the world: "See what science can do? It has ended the war without shedding a drop of blood!"

I was positive then, and I am positive now, that we made a mistake dropping the bomb without a previous bloodless demonstration. But I am quite willing to work on such a project again because I believe that in a democratic government such mistakes are the exception rather than the rule.

To abstain from progress is a medieval idea. I am in favor of any advance in knowledge or any development of the greater power of man. I believe in such advances because I feel that on the whole they will be used in the right way by democratic nations.

Does a scientist have a choice? In an emergency, it is obvious that everyone's choice is more restricted. The pressures are greatly increased. Everyone's responsibility is greater. However, an emergency does not eliminate any individual's responsibility, choice, or conscience.

I am confident that, whatever the scientists are able to discover or invent, the people will be good enough and wise enough to control it for the ultimate benefit of everyone.

U THANT

U Thant is the third Secretary-General of the United Nations. The first was Trygve Lie of Norway, who resigned; the second, Dag Hammarskjold of Sweden, who died in an airplane crash in Africa.

Born in Burma in 1909, the son of a prosperous rice miller, U Thant graduated from Rangoon University. He went on to become a teacher, educator, and writer, before entering politics after World War II. In 1957 he became Burma's chief representative to the UN. In 1959 he was made Vice-President of the General Assembly, and two years later he became Secretary-General.

The Secretary-General is a quiet, soft-spoken, friendly man, trained in the Buddhist tradition of concentration and meditation. He is the right man to head an organization of peace-loving nations who are not exactly at peace with each other. He has used his persuasive and detached efforts to relieve many tense confrontations. He was effective during the Cuban missile crisis and the Congo troubles and, recently, in restoring peace, even if a shaky one, between the Israelis and Arabs.

His name is Thant. The *U* is a title of respect that has no equivalent in English. At UN Headquarters he dresses in an impeccable, dark business suit. In his Manhattan apartment he wears the long Burmese kilt, called a *longyi*.

A devout Buddhist, U Thant saves some part of each day for meditation, to achieve that serenity so badly needed by the man who stands impartially between East and West. So quiet he is, he can use resolute language.

· · · · ·

The United Nations as such has no "face" to lose and no victory of its own to win—it is simply an organization serving all nations but dominated by none.

The maintenance of peace is, of course, our most important task, for a nuclear war could wipe out the world. But there are other grave problems—poverty, hunger, ignorance, disease, injustice—which concern us almost as deeply.

Anybody who proposes the use of atomic weapons for destructive purposes is, in my view, out of his mind.

The United Nations . . . is weak and inadequate but it is still the best hope for getting out of our intolerably dangerous thermonuclear jungle and for creating the beginning of a civilized international community.

No country in the world has permanent friends or permanent interests.

One remarkable feature of the cold war is that each side is so completely convinced of its own rightness. . . Each side is convinced that it alone represents the true philosophy of peace and that the other side is a warmonger.

Let us hope . . . that the kind of national claims and counter claims, colonialism, and imperial wars which characterized the discovery of the earth will not mark the exploration of outer space.

How are we to practice tolerance? What states of mind are necessary for all of us to live together in peace with one another as good neighbors? . . . The answers to these questions lie, it seems to me, in our ability to bring out the best in us and to return to the basic moral and ethical principles of all great religions.

The perpetuation of poverty in a world of plenty is morally wrong and politically intolerable.

Technology can be the most powerful force in the world for raising living standards, and our task is to harness it for that purpose.

A general rise in the standards of education is surely the most effective means of achieving . . . those social transformations that are necessary.

The United Nations stands for the self-government and independence of all peoples, and the abolition of racial discrimination without reservations.

Every human being, of whatever origin, of whatever station, deserves respect. We must each respect others even as we respect ourselves.

HARRY S. TRUMAN

☙ *On May 8, 1884, in honor of the birth of his first son,*
Harry, John Truman, a horse-and-mule trader of
Lamar, Missouri, nailed a horseshoe over the front door of
the little white cottage in which he lived. The horseshoe
and the cottage can still be seen in Lamar . . . but Harry
moved on to the White House.

In between, Harry was a washer of bottles, a wrapper of
newspapers, a timekeeper on a railroad construction job,
and a bookkeeper in a bank. He was also a farmer, a postmaster, an army captain in World War I, a bankrupt haber-
dasher, a county judge, a Senator, and Vice-President of the
United States.

In 1945, when President Franklin D. Roosevelt suddenly
died, Vice-President Truman succeeded to the office. Some
people doubted that Harry Truman could fill the great
President's shoes, but in fact, he turned out to be a coura-
geous leader, who ably guided his country throughout the
difficult postwar years.

Here is his record: he made the heavy decision to use the
atomic bomb against Japan, thus bringing the war in the
East to a close, although he had only learned of the
weapon's existence thirteen days after he became President.

He offered economic and military assistance to Greece and Turkey, established the Marshall Plan to reconstruct devastated Europe, and led the United States into the North Atlantic Treaty Organization, a bulwark against Communist expansion. He stood up against Communist aggression in Korea and, while the war was still raging, dismissed one of this country's great generals, Douglas MacArthur, for insubordination.

In 1948, when his term of office ended, the polls, the radio commentators, and the newspapers predicted that he would not be reelected. Truman stumped the country, talked to the people as one of them, and won their hearts and their votes. *The Washington Post*, which had been against him, draped a big sign over their building saying, "Mr. President, we'll eat crow." Truman sent word to them to take the sign down.

His middle initial S stands for nothing. His parents thought it would be more dignified if Harry had a middle name, so they gave him an S.

. . . . .

We faced half a million casualties trying to take Japan by land. It was either that or the atom bomb, and I didn't hesitate a minute, and I've never lost any sleep over it since.

All my life, whenever it comes time to make a decision, I make it and forget about it.

Delay is decay.

The presidency is the toughest job in the world, and it's

getting tougher as time goes on. But if you work at it all the time, every day, and don't let the hard decisions pile up on you, it won't get you down.

The more people know and understand their government, the better government they will have.

I don't have any sympathy with anyone who complains about what's done when he never takes any interest in it.

No president can really select his successor, although most presidents—being in control of the party machinery—try to do it.

The man who insists on seeing all sides [of a problem] often can't make up his mind where to take hold.

The Southerners are just as fine a people as you will find anywhere in the nation, and when they come to the conclusion that race and creed and color don't make any difference in what's in a man's heart, then we won't have any trouble.

Many books written by generals since time began seem to me to be mainly alibis.

I come from a religious family and we believe in the efficacy of prayer.

I never had the complex of being a big shot, and I prefer my life in Missouri.

I said somewhere or other in a speech that I might run for the Senate again when I'm 91. A few days later I got a letter from a fellow who said he had looked it up, and that that wouldn't be an election year. So maybe I'll push it ahead and run when I'm 90.

(A little sign that used to be on his desk in the White House read:) The Buck Stops Here.

NORBERT WIENER

American mathematician, social philosopher, teacher, and author of science fiction. A child prodigy, he graduated from college, receiving his B.A. at the age of fourteen. He received his Ph.D. at Harvard at the age of eighteen. He later studied at Cornell, Columbia, and Cambridge, in Copenhagen, and in Göttingen, Germany.

Wiener was born in Columbia, Missouri, in 1894, the son of a self-made professor of Slavic languages from Russia. His early education was at home, his father taking an acute interest in his studies. Wiener's views on social issues reflected those that were held by his father, the liberal views of Tolstoi.

At twenty-five he joined the Mathematics Department of the Massachusetts Institute of Technology, where he served until his retirement at the age of sixty-six.

He was chiefly concerned with the problems of how man and machines can live together. He was the founder of the science of *cybernetics,* a study of common principles involved in the functions of computers and of the human nervous system. During World War II Wiener developed improvement in radar and in antiaircraft projectiles. He died in 1964.

. . . . .

When I give an order to a machine, the situation is not essentially different from that which arises when I give an order to a person.

Certain analogies of behavior are being observed between the machine and the living organism.

The nervous system and the automatic machine are fundamentally alike in that they are devices which make decisions on the basis of decisions they have made in the past.

The average American child of the upper middle class . . . is brought up in an atmosphere of Santa Claus; and when he learns that Santa Claus is a myth, he cries bitterly . . . and spends much of his later life in the search for some emotional substitute.

If we compare man with the great apes, his closest relatives, we find that mature man in hair, head, shape, body proportions, bone structure, muscles, and so on, is more like a newborn ape than the adult ape. Among the animals, man is a Peter Pan who never grows up.

This immaturity of anatomical structure corresponds to man's prolonged childhood.

The young chimpanzee is extraordinarily like a child, and clearly his equal or perhaps his superior in intellectual matters.

Fortunately, or unfortunately as the case may be, most chimpanzees . . . persist in being good chimpanzees, and do not become quasi-human morons.

If a child does not walk until it is three or four years old, it may have lost all the desire to walk. Ordinary locomotion may become a harder task than driving a car for the normal adult.

One lion's roar is very nearly another lion's roar. Yet there are animals such as the parrot, the myna, and the crow, which seem to be able to pick up sounds from the surrounding environment. . . . The birds that can imitate human speech have several characteristics in common: they are social, they are rather long-lived, and they have memories which are excellent.

It is quite possible for a person to talk to a machine, a machine to a person, and a machine to a machine.

When an invention is made, a considerable period generally elapses before its full implications are understood. . . . The effect of atomic energy on mankind and the future is yet to be assessed.

The radio-telephone had achieved the stature of the radio-telegraph, and . . . broadcasting was possible. Let not the fact that this great triumph of invention has largely been given over to the soap opera and the hillbilly singer blind one to the excellent work that was done in developing it.

When I say that the machine's danger to society is not from the machine itself but from what man makes of it. . . .

There is one quality more important than "know-how" . . . this is "know-what" by which we determine not only how to accomplish our purposes, but what our purposes are to be.

In the myths and fairy tales we read as children we learned a few truths of life, such has that when a djinnee is found in a bottle, it had better be left there.

If you are given three wishes, you must be very careful what you wish for.

We have modified our environment so radically that we must now modify ourselves to exist in this new environment.

The hour is very late, and the choice of good and evil knocks at our door.

ROY WILKINS

☥ | *Negro leader, executive secretary of the National Association for the Advancement of Colored People.* The purpose of this organization, founded in 1909 and generally referred to by its initials NAACP, is to assist the black community in achieving its rights in every field of human endeavor—housing, voting, working, education, public accommodation.

Roy Wilkins was born in St. Louis in 1901, the grandson of a Mississippi slave. His mother died of tuberculosis, and because his father was unable to support the family, Roy was reared by an aunt and uncle in St. Paul in a racially mixed, broken-down neighborhood. To help pay for his studies, Roy worked as a redcap in St. Paul's Union Station, and as a dining-car waiter on the Northern Pacific. He also worked on a clean-up squad at the South St. Paul stockyards.

Many such poor Negro boys worked hard to keep body and soul together while going to school.

After graduation from college, Wilkins became a journalist and got a job in Kansas City on the miltant Negro weekly, *Call*. In those early days the most urgent problem was the fight against lynching. Between 1888 and 1918 it is estimated that 3,224 Negroes were hanged, burned, or otherwise murdered.

Wilkins worked for eight years as a reporter and managing editor at *Call*. He has been a full-time worker for NAACP for thirty-eighty years. A tall, lean, quiet man, he is a low-keyed speaker, in direct contrast with professional rabblerousers. His fragile health does not keep him from working fourteen hours a day.

. . . . .

Sure, young people pressure us. I welcome it, many young Negroes today don't know the history of the fight to end segregation.

Kansas City ate my heart out. It was a Jim Crow town through and through. There were two school systems, bad housing, police brutality, bombings in Negro neighborhoods. Police were arresting white and Negro high school kids just for being together. The legitmate theater saved half of the last row in the top balcony for Negroes. If the show was bad, they gave us two rows.

We had to stop lynching because they were killing us. We had to provide physical security.

We have completely changed the thinking of the country on lynching. At one time it was defended in the Senate, and even in the pulpit. There is no comparison now with the fear we once knew.

The Negro citizen has come to the point where he is not

afraid of violence. He no longer shrinks back. He will assert himself, and if violence comes, so be it.

Demonstrations are like prepping a patient for surgery. They often serve to get a community ready, and then we can move in without other approaches.

We have stuck to our knitting and used all our weapons.

Wherever Gandhi's techniques fit, they can be used. But it must be remembered that in India the Indian was in the majority; he could stop the country. In the U.S., the Negro is in the minority; he can't stop anything very long.

Our association does not believe a white person should be discharged to make room for a Negro.

It's really thrilling and exciting to be a Negro in the 60's. The whole gamut of Negro life is an adventure if you can roll with the punches and not let it get you into the valley of bitterness. I've never been motivated by any persistent strong feeling against white people. Thank God.

White people are like colored. They are glad and sad. They know poverty and trouble and divorce and sickness. I may be an incurable optimist, but I believe there are more people who want to do good than do evil. The Negro couldn't have made it without the help of some white people.

You can't keep a man in a ditch without staying in there with him. White people have been prisoners of this situation, just as we have been. The whites living today didn't cause it and neither did we, but the whites sustain it because it's comfortable and profitable.

The back of segregation is broken. A whole new era is before us. This will be a period when the Negro will have to make readjustments. We must counsel our Negro population on induction into an integrated society, teach them that you can't blame all disabilities on race, because this is self-defeating.

A great number of Negroes are ready for all their rights now. A great number are not fully aware of the competition and responsibility which await them in an unsegregated world.

There's going to be ice cream and mortgages and taxes, and all the things that whites have in their world, and tedium too. It's not going to be heaven.

If we can underwrite the economies of Germany, France, Italy, and England and see that these people recover their equilibrium, then we can underwrite the cost of recovering the equilibrium of our own native black people.

WHITNEY M. YOUNG, JR.

⚓ *Young, a suave, elegant Negro, is executive director of the National Urban League, an organization formed* to assist Negroes in the cities by creating better living conditions, better job opportunities, and respect for their human rights. In one year alone the Urban League found jobs for 40,000 unemployed Negroes.

Young is not an example of the poor boy who made good. His father was president of the Lincoln Institute, a white-administered school for Negroes in Lincoln Ridge, Kentucky. His mother was the first Negro postmistress of Lincoln Ridge.

Whitney studied under a white tutor and got straight A's, graduating at fourteen. He also got high grades at the segregated Kentucky State College.

In World War II Young enlisted, and was sent to the Massachusetts Institute of Technology for a course in electrical engineering. Despite his education, he then went to Europe as an enlisted man in a Negro road-construction company.

After the war he helped to organize the Congress of Racial Equality, known as CORE, and before joining the National Urban League he worked for the National Association for the Advancement of Colored People. He turned down a $75,000-a-year vice-presidency with one corporation to keep a less remunerative job at the Urban League.

He does not believe that burning down the cities and looting the department stores would create better living conditions for Negroes. Rather, he believes in cooperation between blacks and whites.

In 1966 he visited Pope Paul VI in Rome and, in a fifteen-minute audience, promoted a papal encyclical on racial injustice.

Negro extremists sometimes label him an Uncle Tom—an insulting name, meaning compromiser. Young's reply is: "I'm prepared to be a Tom if it's the only way I can save women and children from being shot down in the street."

. . . . .

Whether the moderates can prevail will be determined by whether there is an immediate and tangible response to the riots from the white community.

You've got to give us some victories.

It isn't a question of moderate versus militant, but of responsibility versus irresponsibility, sanity versus insanity, effectiveness versus ineffectiveness.

You can holler, protest, march, picket, and demonstrate, but somebody must be able to sit in on the strategy conferences and plot a course.

The most important thing that we do is still to get jobs for people. "Green Power" is important for the Negro now.

Pride and dignity come when you reach in your pocket and find money, not a hole.

Anybody can get a bi-racial commission together after a riot. The League provides an opportunity for dialogue and candid discussion before the riot.

The lower middle class in America thinks that status means exclusiveness, that those white, antiseptic ghettos called suburbs are the place to go. We need a generation of people who have the commitment and creativity to try integration —to explore the creative possibilties of diversity.

I don't think it rests in the hands of the Negro. He has already said in a thousand ways that he believes in America. Now the time has come for America to say, "I believe in you."

BIBLIOGRAPHY

☥ | *The author wishes to acknowledge that the following*
     sources were helpful to him in the preparation of this
book:

Brown, Leonard, editor. *A Quarto of Modern Literature.*
New York: Charles Scribner's Sons, 1957.
Cahn, William. *Einstein.* New York: Citadel Press, 1955.
Clark, Glenn. *The Man Who Talks with the Flowers.* St.
Paul, Minnesota: Macalester Park Publishing Com-
pany, 1939.
Copland, Aaron. *What to Listen for in Music.* New York:
McGraw-Hill Book Company, 1939.
Esar, Evan, editor. *Dictionary of Humorous Quotations.*
New York: Horizon Press, Inc., 1949.
Freud, Sigmund. *The Basic Writings of Sigmund Freud.*
New York: The Modern Library, Random House,
Inc., 1938.
Gandhi, Mohandas K. *Autobiography.* Washington, D.C.:
Public Affairs Press, 1948.
Goldman, Alex J. *The Quotable Kennedy.* New York: Bel-
mont Books, 1967.
Goldwater, Robert, and Treves, Marco. *Artists on Art.*
New York: Pantheon Books, Inc., 1945.
Hesse, Hermann. *The Journey to the East.* New York:
Farrar, Straus & Giroux, Inc., 1957.
Hesse, Hermann. *Magister Ludi.* New York: Frederick
Ungar Publishing Company, Inc., 1949.
Hesse, Hermann. *Steppenwolf.* New York: Holt, Rinehart
& Winston, Inc., 1964.

Hicks, Wilson, and Soule, Gardner. *This Is Ike.* New York: Holt, Rinehart & Winston, Inc., 1952.

John XXIII, Pope. *Wit and Wisdom of Good Pope John,* edited by Henri Fesquet. New York: P. J. Kenedy & Sons, 1964.

Life, the editors of. *Winston Churchill.* 1965.

Lin Yutang. *My Country and My People.* New York: The John Day Company, Inc., 1935.

Lorant, Stefan. *FDR, A Pictorial Biography.* New York: Simon & Schuster, Inc., 1950.

McLuhan, Marshall. *The Medium Is the Message.* New York: Bantam Books, Inc., 1967.

Mead, Margaret. *People and Places.* Cleveland, Ohio: The World Publishing Company, 1959.

Meir, Golda. *This Is Our Strength.* New York: The Macmillan Company, 1962.

A Marianne Moore Reader. New York: Viking Press, Inc., 1961.

Nehru on Gandhi. New York: The John Day Company, Inc., 1948.

Niebuhr, Reinhold. *Does Civilization Need Religion?* New York: The Macmillan Company, 1928.

Niebuhr, Reinhold. *Moral Man and Immoral Society.* New York: Charles Scribner's Sons, 1932.

Niebuhr, Reinhold. *The Social Sources of Denominationalism.* New York: Holt, Rinehart & Winston, Inc., 1929.

Pandit, Vijaya Lakshmi. *The Evolution of India.* Plymouth, England: Bowering Press, 1958.

Roosevelt, Eleanor. *Book of Common Sense Etiquette.* New York: The Macmillan Company, 1962.

Russell, Bertrand. *The Autobiography of Bertrand Russell, 1914-1944.* Boston: Atlantic Monthly Press; Little, Brown, 1967.

Russell, Bertrand. *The Practice and Theory of Bolshevism.* New York: Simon & Schuster, Inc., 1964.

Russell, Bertrand. *Unpopular Essays.* New York: Simon & Schuster, Inc., 1950.

Russell, Bertrand. *The Wisdom of Bertrand Russell.* New York: Philosophical Library, 1968.

Schlesinger, Arthur M., Jr. *A Thousand Days.* Boston: Houghton Mifflin Company, 1965.

Schweitzer, Albert. *Out of My Life and Thought.* New York: Holt, Rinehart & Winston, Inc., 1949.

Shaw, George Bernard. *Everybody's Political What's What?* London: Constable and Company, Ltd., 1944.

Sorenson, Theodore C. *Kennedy.* New York: Harper & Row Publishers, Inc., 1965.

Stein, Gertrude. *Writings and Lectures, 1911-1945.* New York: Random House, Inc., 1941.

Thomas, Henry, and Thomas, Dana Lee. *50 Great Modern Lives.* Hanover House, 1956.

Thruelson, R., and Kober, J., editors. *Adventures of the Mind.* Saturday Evening Post; Alfred A. Knopf, Inc., 1959.

Wiener, Norbert. *The Human Use of Human Beings.* Boston: Houghton Mifflin Co.

A dictionary of *Existentialism.* New York: The Wisdom Library, 1960.

Freedom & Union, Clarence Streit, publisher.

Homage to a Friend. United States Committee for the United Nations, 1964.

The Secretary-General Speaks, United Nations, OPI.

The Hindu, Madras, India.

Life Magazine   *Newsweek* Magazine
Look Magazine   *Time* Magazine
The New York Times, Book Review
The New York Times, Daily
The New York Times, Magazine

INDEX